Cdste
Wilkerson

Preaching in/and the Borderlands

Preaching *in*/*and* the Borderlands

EDITED BY

J. Dwayne Howell AND
Charles L. Aaron Jr.

PICKWICK *Publications* · Eugene, Oregon

PREACHING IN/AND THE BORDERLANDS

Pickwick Publications
An Imprint of Wipf and Stock Publishers
199 W. 8th Ave., Suite 3
Eugene, OR 97401

www.wipfandstock.com

PAPERBACK ISBN: 978-1-5326-6465-6
HARDCOVER ISBN: 978-1-5326-6466-3
EBOOK ISBN: 978-1-5326-6467-0

Cataloguing-in-Publication data:

Names: Howell, J. Dwayne, editor. | Aaron, Charles L., Jr., editor.

Title: Preaching in/and the borderlands / edited by J. Dwayne Howell and Charles L. Aaron Jr.

Description: Eugene, OR: Pickwick Publications, 2020. | Includes bibliographical references.

Identifiers: ISBN 978-1-5326-6465-6 (paperback). | ISBN 978-1-5326-6466-3 (hardcover). | ISBN 978-1-5326-6467-0 (ebook).

Subjects: LCSH: Preaching. |Emigration and Immigration—Relgious aspects—Christianity.

Classification: BR517 P85 2020 (print). | BR517 (ebook).

The Reverend Rachel Griffin Baughman, Senior Pastor, and
the staff and members of Oak Lawn United Methodist Church
in Dallas, Texas, whose ministry on behalf of the sojourner
embodies the spirit of the book.

In memory of the Reverend Barney Ferguson,
who taught me as a youth what it means to care about
the needs of others.

Contents

Preface / xi

List of Contributors / xv

Poem: "They Cross the Border" / Harold Recinos / xviii

1 This Is Just the End: On How not to Go Mad These Days
  / *Cláudio Carvalhae*s / 1

2 Why I'm Here / *Miguel A. De La Torre* / 15

3 Being White These Days / *Robert P. Hoch* / 25

4 Making U.S. Protestant Disciples of ALL Nations
  / *Gerald C. Liu* / 41

5 An Overview of the Current Landscape of Immigration Law
  / *Sarah Ellen Eads Adkins* / 51

6 Immigration and the Biblical Migrant Narratives
  / *J. Dwayne Howell* / 66

7 Turning Cheeks at Checkpoints: Matthew 5:38–48 as a Text of
  Terror or Expression of Encouragement for Immigrant Audiences?
  / *Melanie A. Howard* / 79

8 Moving from Caution to Faithful Proclamation:
  One Pastor's Story / *Owen K. Ross* / 92

9 Toward a Border-Crossing Homiletic: Building Blocks
   for Trauma-Informed Preaching Practices / *Lis Valle* / 107

10 Comrades of the Kin-dom / *Rebecca David Hensley* / 119

11 God's Kingdom at the Border / *Michael W. Waters* / 127

12 Wounded Enough for Some to Believe / *Heidi Neumar*k / 133

13 Immigration Ministry through Relationships *Rhonda Thompson* / 136

14 By God's Grace: Stumbling into Multi–Cultural Ministry and
    Lesson Learned / *Jason Crosby* / 149

    Bibliography / 161

Preface

"You shall love the immigrant as yourself" (Lev 19:34). These words struck me as I taught a class at Campbellsville University. First, because the passage is paralleled to Lev 19:18, "You shall love your neighbor as yourself." Secondly, it was just after 9/11 and the nation witnessed the xenophobia that emerged out of the tragedy. It is shocking to see fear turn to hatred and blame often directed toward immigrants and those of foreign descent. Even as I write today, we are witnessing the abuse of those of Asian lineage during the Covid-19 pandemic. In the present political atmosphere immigrants are turned away at the border, children are locked in cages, and walls are being built. Immigration is strongly debated in American society including the church.

What is to be the Church's response to the immigrant? This is a question I have asked in both my classes and in church study groups. Most immigrants in American society are seeking a better life. They are among the most vulnerable, possessing little and at the mercy of those they work for and in the communities where they live. Leviticus 19:33 and 34 reminds us that we are not to harm the immigrant and we are to treat the immigrant as a citizen, literally like a "well planted tree." The essays in this book address issues for churches to consider as they seek to better understand how to respond to immigration. I want to thank Charles Aaron for offering me the opportunity to co-edit this book.

This book took shape during planning for the 2016 meeting of the Society of Biblical Literature, within the Homiletics and Biblical Studies program unit. That session of SBL met in San Antonio, Texas. Dr. David Schnasa Jacobsen, Bishops Scholar in Homiletics and Preaching at Boston University School of Theology, suggested the theme of preaching and immigration. With Texas on the front lines of immigration battles, the rest of the group enthusiastically agreed with the suggestion, and the working title of the panel presentation: "Preaching In/And the Borderlands." Texas represented the border between Mexico and the United States, at the heart of the immigration controversies. We quickly realized how much biblical material—narrative, law, parable—involved immigration. We had found a topic timely, important, and thoroughly embedded in every genre of the biblical writings. We knew that we needed a widely diverse panel, with many perspectives. After we had assembled the panel, Dwayne Howell and Charles Aaron knew that the papers for this panel had to exert an influence beyond the brief two hours of the presentation in San Antonio. We readily agreed to produce this book, adding authors and insights from different fields. We wanted a book that examined the academic background of the biblical, ethical, theological and homiletical disciplines. We also wanted a book with contributions from experienced pastors, legal experts, and activists. After many years and a few delays, we feel honored to offer you this volume.

This book is divided into four sections. The first section addresses ethical and legal areas of immigration with essays written by Cláudio Carvalhaes, Miguel De La Torre, Robert P. Hoch, Gerald C. Liu and Sarah Ellen Eads Adkins. In the next section J. Dwayne Howell and Melanie A. Howard provide examples of how both the Old Testament and New Testament speak to immigration. The third section offers essays on homiletic concepts on preaching about immigration by Owen K. Ross and Lis Valle followed by three sermons by Rebecca David Hensley, Michael W. Waters, and Heidi Neumark. The final section provides stories by Rhonda Thompson and Jason Crosby about how ministries to immigrant communities have been incorporated into local churches in Montgomery, Alabama, and Louisville, Kentucky.

The editors would like to thank the other members of the Program Unit (official and unofficial) who helped with every aspect of producing this book. They invited panelists, who turned into contributors, and made suggestions for other people who could help with the book. They also performed all of the yeoman duties for putting together a panel. The members of the steering committee include Eunjoo Kim of Iliff School of Theology,

Alyce McKenzie and Wesley Allen of Perkins School of Theology, Karoline Lewis and Joy J. Moore of Luther Seminary, Carolyn J. Sharp of Yale Divinity School, Ruthanna Hooke of Virginia Theological Seminary, and the aforementioned David Jacobsen. We offer our appreciation for all that you did to make this book a reality.

We likewise want to thank Pickwick Publications and our editors, Daniel Lanning and George Callihan, for providing the opportunity and the guidance for us to publish this work.

J. Dwayne Howell
Campbellsville, KY
Easter 2020

Charles L. Aaron
Dallas, TX
Easter 2020

Contributors

Charles L. Aaron, Jr., coeditor
Codirector of the Intern Program
Perkins School of Theology
Southern Methodist University
Dallas, TX

Sarah Ellen Eads Adkins
Executive Director
Neighbors Immigration Clinic
Lexington, KY

Claudio Carvalhaes
Associate Professor of Worship
Union Theological Seminary
New York, NY

Jason Crosby
Copastor
Crescent Hill Baptist Church
Louisville, KY

Miguel A. De La Torre
Professor of Social Ethics and Latinx Studies
Iliff School of Theology
Denver, CO

Becky David Hensley
PhD Student, Joint Doctoral Program in the Study of Religion
University of Denver/Iliff School of Theology
Denver, CO

Robert Hoch
Pastor
First and Franklin Presbyterian Church
Baltimore, MD

Melanie A. Howard
Assistant Professor of Biblical and Religious Studies
Fresno Pacific University
Fresno, CA

J. Dwayne Howell, coeditor
Professor Emeritus of Old Testament and Hebrew
Campbellsville University
Campbellsville, KY

Gerald C. Liu
Assistant Professor of Worship & Preaching
Princeton Theological Seminary
Princeton, NJ

Heidi Neumark
Pastor
Trinity Lutheran Church/Iglesia Luterana Trinidada
New York, NY

Harold J. Recinos
Professor of Church and Society
Perkins School of Theology,
Southern Methodist University
Dallas, TX

Owen K. Ross
Director of Church Development
North Texas Annual Conference of the United Methodist Church

Rhonda Thompson
Director, The Nehemiah Center
First Baptist Church, Montgomery
Montgomery, AL

Lis Valle
Assistant Professor of Homiletics
McCormick Theological Seminary
Chicago, IL

Michael Waters
Pastor
Joy Tabernacle AME Church
Dallas, TX

They Cross the Border

HAROLD J. RECINOS

they travel with homes stuffed
into small bags, sleep in fields,

on hard dirt floors, bus station
benches, on tractor trains, beside

the rivers that have for centuries
rounded hills, and beneath distant

stars hanging like lanterns in an
ancient sky. along the underground

railroad on the long walk toward the
border, light on the walls of Spanish

speaking shacks open their eyes to
the simple frailty of life, the voices

fled in grief, the choking feeling in
the company of other women and

children walking away from endless
poverty and violence that they will

be changed and their children by the
year's end no longer recognized. in

lucid moments they stare at evening
stars blinking stories of hate waiting

to include them at the border, offering
quiet prayers to God who hides in the

black patches between dots of celestial
light forgetting to comfort them. they

have ambled Sunday shoes dark in less
than forty days, El Norte drawing near

with each brown step, children insisting
with occasional tears they can keep the

pace, giving illness in their long days
another name, trying to reach America
scrubbed fresh with dreams, hoping when
they come up against the southern wall

they are not named poison, or living filth
by the Lilly white people living behind

the locked door who stopped emptying
their years of memories made complete

on the land whose border their names
crossed to become another country

1

This Is Just the End

On How not to Go Mad These Days[1]

—CLÁUDIO CARVALHAES

> You see all these buildings, do you not? Truly I tell you, not one stone will be left here upon another; all will be thrown down . . . Beware that no one leads you astray . . . *And you will hear of wars and rumors of war*s; see that you are not alarmed . . . all this is but the beginning of the birth pangs. 'Then they will hand you over to be tortured and will put you to death. Many will fall away, and they will betray one another and hate one another. And many false prophets will arise and lead many astray. And because of the increase of lawlessness, the love of many will grow cold. But anyone who endures to the end will be saved. we raise our voices together and hold each other hands[2]

I have been telling my family and my friends that it is good to be here with my Latinxs community as we see and hear about all of the disasters and horrors done to our people at the borders. Better to be together, to cry together, to go mad together, to sing and pray together, to draw near each other in some form of warmth and solidarity! The brutal immigration policy separating children from their parents and then putting them up for

---

1. This sermon-article combines two sermons with newer annotations preached at the Hispanic Summer Program 2018 at Perkins School of Theology, Dallas, Texas, in June 2018.

2. Matt 24: 1–14, NRSV.

adoption showed us again what this country is made of. Something that the indigenous and the black people of this country already knew way too well. With this uproar against immigrants and especially the Latinxs people, it seems that it is becoming clearer for other people that:

1. We, minority people, live in a viciously angry, merciless and racist country.

2. That the State rules with clear *necro-politics* of ethnic cleansing.

3. That our identity is that of a foreigner, socially placed at the borderlands, politically placed in the hatred of Republicans and awkwardness of Democrats, religiously placed in old forms of Catholicism, Pentecostal naiveté, and folk mythic beliefs, and psychologically located at the borderline of feelings between madness and lunacy.

4. That the nationalist rhetoric in the United States pivots away from brownness to construct a reality of pan-criminalization for all racialized brown bodied people. Today in the US, to be brown bodied is to be a Muslim-Hindu-Christian-immigrant-mexican-central-american-terriorist-rapist-low-skilled-poor-drug-dealer-illegal-dependent-animal.

5. Our people, immigrants, undocumented, have become the fake news of the content of the president "emergency declaration"!

We see churches and Christian institutions trying hard to learn how to deal with us but at the end, we are always at the tail end of respect, processes of decision, abilities, gifts to offer. The amount of solidarity offered, with important exceptions, is proportional to its expendable resources, guilt and not knowing.

The people at the border are for many, an unfortunate calamity. The distancing from these immigrants at the borders reflects the ongoing distance between white churches and the Latinxs communities. For many institutions, this immigrant disaster is mostly an occasion for a robust declaration against its situation and nothing else. What is always at stake is fear, self-protection, and self-interest. This situation is derivative of the discourse around blacks and whites in this country where other minorities have a hard time pinching in in some more fundamental ways. White supremacy continues to hold on to power, hide its brutalities in administrative legalities, business proper, law and order, state theology and political paraphernalia. All of this done in the name of Jesus!

The hidden perversity of the pleasure of seeing the pain of the children behind cages ripped away from their parents is beyond words. The system of immigration is indeed broken in its fullness when the government does not know how to get the kids back to their parents, when little children have to go to court to respond to judges about the conditions of their immigration status when all that they want is to play with toys and call for their *mamas y papas*.

Maddening! Whoever is not getting mad with these series of dreadful events are not paying attention, are not seriously taking the position of those parents living in unspeakable pain. We must take their side for their children are our children! So, we must return them to their parents and not to put them up for adoption! It is as if my precious children were in jail and I am rendered completely powerless to do anything. It is as if my kids have been taken away from me and I do not even know where to start to get them back. The situation of loss is such that at a certain point one might even start to imagine that their kids would be better off dead or with somebody else who will take care of them. If our hearts don't drop to the floor when we see a child estranged from her mama because she hasn't seen her for months and then seeing pure panic in the face of this mother, we are definitely not paying attention. Our hearts have already been covered by numbness, by privilege, the Spirit of God has left us and the gospel lost its place in our life. "Woe to those who plan iniquity, to those who plot evil on their beds! At morning's light they carry it out because it is in their power to do it." (Micah 2:1). Moreover, I think we Latinxs need a new translation for the Psalm 139. One that goes this way:

1   O God, you have searched us and known us well.

2   You know when we cross the desert and when we swim through the Rio Grande;

    you discern our fears from far away.

3   You search out the path of our people, the immigrants,

    in the desert, you find all of the shoes, toothbrushes, underwear, crucifixes,

    and the blood of our people.

    in prisons, you find our children alone, completely lost, and parents with a hole so

    great in their hearts that they are swallowed by grief.

    You are acquainted with all our desperation.

3

4   Even before a word is on our tongue, or a tear is shed

O God, you know us so completely. You know we are lost for words here.

5   like the heat of the desert and the cold water of Rio Grande you surround us.

6   Such knowledge is too wonderful for us;

we believe in you so much, you wouldn't believe it.

7   Where can we go to find your Spirit?

we go to El Norte fleeing from hunger, violence and devastations,

where can we find the security of your presence?

8   If we knock at the doors of churches, we never know if we will be welcomed or they

will call La Migra;

if we try to go to Christian seminaries you will not be there.

For they are afraid of their statues and only concerned with their deep thoughts and research.

9   If we take the wings of the morning,

and go fight on the streets for our people,

they will come with the police and their laws and put us in jail

10 We wished your hand could lead us,

protect us, and hold us fast. But we have nothing.

11 For if we say, 'Surely the darkness shall cover me,

and the light around us become night',

12 Darkness we are;

We are the night that shines as the day,

We are darkness to the world

and to You too."

Our time can be defined as a time of white supremacy dominion, millionaires and billionaires as political representatives, global regulation by hydro/agri-business, and brutal state control grounded on an endless state of exception that sanctions all forms of violence, the reality of the Empire is translated into a) a myriad of fears wrapped up in patriotism and religious certainties; b) the sooner death of the earth and c) a constant war on women, the poor, indigenous, black and brown bodies.

During such a time as this, when our borderlands are a sign of death, we raise our voices together and hold each other's hands. When violence separates *ninos y ninas de sus mamas y papas*, we raise our voices together and hold each other hands. When border crossers are turned into unlawful people who are then prosecuted and have to plead guilty when they are NOT guilty of anything, we raise our voices together and hold each other's hands. When violence forcibly injects psychotropic in our children as we hear reports from New Orleans of a 9-year-old boy who was kept in a children concentration camp and tried to run away. When a boy is then sent to the Shiloh Treatment Center in Texas and the doctor creates a narrative that says he needs psychotropic medication so he is drugged and tamed. His mother has no idea what is happening to her son. We raise our voices together and hold each other's hands

When violence kidnaps our children in the midst of the night to be trafficked as we could see it in a video done by New York One TV in New York city, both cases were denounced by Democracy Now! We raise our voices together and hold each other's hands.

This is the United States of America today! This is American fascism through bio-power and *necro-politics* fully lived at the borderland in the bodies of brown people! For we are not only the people who live in the borderland, we are the borderland. Thus friends, I must say, we have to place our personal suffering in perspective when we are dealing with this much bigger threat to our lives. We need empathy for our own people. We need to take a step further them, which can be a step away from where we are right now.

I pray to Jesus who said to not be alarmed . . . But in my prayer, I say Jesus, how can we not be alarmed? They are coming in the night; they are coming in the morning. *How do we not go mad with all this?* Here are some things for us to remember as we go through these times:

First, We Are the Ones Who We Have Been Waiting For

We can't wait for anyone! Not even for God! For most of our theologies are traps that paralyze us and nurture us with fear and as I said, we don't have many institutions to back us up and protect our lives. We can't wait for anybody to come and rescue us. Like Job, we must find a way through our suffering within ourselves and our communities. The only way Jesus will come to us will be thorough each other and some friends. There is no big leader or an assortment of "they" that will come to us to save us. Jennifer Harvey rightfully says:

> There is no all-powerful "they" out there who is going to swoop in and stop this. There is no one coming to end these injustices and degradations once-and-for-all. I have to admit something. Each morning, these days, I wake up, and I realize some part of me is holding my breath in anticipation. I'm hoping, maybe even expecting, this: surely today is the day "they" will come. I am waiting for "them." And when "they" come . . . mothers fleeing war won't lose their babies. And Black people's lives and bodies will be secure. And borders will be exposed as arbitrary while the people who cross them are honored as sacred. And trans and queer people's humanity will no longer be degraded and destroyed, but celebrated and revered. But, beloveds, "they" ARE NOT COMING. There is only you and I and we. You are the one you are waiting for. I am the one I am waiting for. We are the ones we are waiting for (as June Jordan said and Alice Walker cited after). So, we must be that. All of us. Today. Right now. In every moment. In every place. Beloveds . . . there's something else we need to know about we. We are many. And if we really understand who we are waiting for, we are powerful. We can be that. What do we choose?[3]

There is none coming for us. We are the ones we are waiting for!

We Must Be Aware of Our History

It is said that a people who don't know its history tend to repeat it. People who don't know their own history will not be able to see the traps they are caught up in during the present time. People who don't know our history will call the recent history a kind of collective unconscious fate, or destiny, instead of seeing what is happening now is due to our choices and positioning in the past. Knowing our history is to excavate who we are, where we come from and see the ways our being is always an interbeing, always connected with the earth and other people. Knowing our history will help us face the fears that surround us and work on our challenges and mistakes, naming the wrongs we did in the historical processes that defined our trajectory. People who don't know our history tend to not know the difference

3. Harvey, Facebook page, June 15, 2018 at 9:50 AM.

between coloniality and indigeneity, easily confusing their hunter with their savior. People who don't know our history tend to go in two ways: they either can't see specificities, differences and commonalities or they become so self-righteous that they can't see the interrelationality and the blurring lines between traditions and the expansive common belonging of the people. People who don't know our history keep working with the tools of the master's house within the master's house.

Know the Immigrant Reasoning: Don't Fall for the Empire Logic of "Conquer and Divide"

Achille Mbembe, Cameroonian philosopher and political theorist said in *Critique of Black Reason*: "The fierce colonial desire to divide and classify, to create hierarchies and produce difference, leaves behind wounds and scars. Worse, it created a fault line that lives on."[4] We so easily fall prey to this de-classificatory project of undermining our own people, of creating hierarchies of difference, of widening our colonial wounds. Sometimes we don't realize that all we do is to fight for the crumbs we are thrown. We must think that our work is to find a safe space for our community and save it from everyone. NO! We must think ourselves as a collective, as a community, as a cloud of living witness and ancestors, of foreigners and strangers, as people interrelated to many other people and the earth. Latinxs people are made up of Afro-Latinos, indigenous people, Africans, whites, yellows and blacks. As we are made of the earth, animals, sentient and non-sentient beings. To fall prey to a certain politics of identity that erases the earth and makes communities into self-enclosed identities, self-sufficient groups and islands of self-proclaimed safety and self-righteousness, is to became weak, disconnected, debilitated, and confused and to fall prey to a victimhood with self-awareness that weakens our collective struggle and common ways of living. We are many! We are the composition of peoples and ethnicities and animals in many humanities. We cannot be communities atomized into itself and in need to defend its identity territory at any cost, even at the cost of trashing somebody else. We cannot live our identity without the identity of the earth and the animals either. We must call on what Indian literary critic and theorist Gayatri Chakravorty Spivak called "strategic essentialism,"[5] and even expanding it to the earth and all sentient and non-

4. Mbembe, *Critique of Black Reason*, 218–22.

5. Strategic essentialism is "a political tactic employed by a minority group acting on

sentient beings in order to find our commonalities in the common struggle. Instead of feeding a "network of doubling, uncertainty, and equivocation,"[6] we must offer mutual trust, assurances for a collective work done for liberation of people. Where spaces for ambiguities are held together.

Be Aware of Our Own Selves: Circulation and Borderlands

Every single human being is a work of many materials, forms and compositions, entities and voices and belongings. Star dust, our common ground is the universe and the earth, humus, where we all come from. As we inhabit this piece of the land around the world, what distinguishes the Latinxs people, among other things, is the complexities of our borderlands. We inhabit many worlds and none of these worlds are full. We are people of no one country. We are the borderlands, *No somos de aquí ni de allá. Estranamos a todo y todas.* We are in the midst of a state of slumber, numbed, and yet, fully active, fully wired. We are wrestling to understand our walk in the desert, in what poet Paul Valéry called the "leap of no return."[7] In Portuguese *Lonjura sem retorno*, in Spanish: *lejos sin regreso*. We are somewhat, not in the same complexity and specificities, like the African people that, in the words of Mbembe, are marked by "the articulation . . . of a thinking of circulation and crossings.[8] Our circulation is limited, and our bodies crossed by so many borders: economic, sexual, gender, class. The cultural economy of US demands a form of circulation of goods and cultural artifacts and ways of living that tends to detach us from our own circulation of sources of sustenance and communal living. If we don't hold to what we learned from our great grandparents we will not be able to know who we are and engage with awareness and fullness into the newness of the new circulations within this country. As we learn about ourselves and the histories of those from the bottom of this country that we are not part of the American "WE." The American WE is very specific to a group of people, pertaining to a middle upper white class. The WE don't have allegiance to its own white people either, for the real commitment is around

the basis of a shared identity in the public arena in the interests of unity during a struggle for equal rights. The term was coined by Spivak and has been influential in feminism, queer theory, and postcolonial theory."

6. Mbembe, *Critique of Black Reason*, 381.

7. Mbembe, *Critique of Black Reason*, 418–19.

8. Mbembe, *Critique of Black Reason*, 360–62

class compromises. The white trash are not part of the WE of this country either. So, it is a naïve move to try to assimilate with the hopes of belonging. Trump's America has its greatness to his own people. Make American Great Again, MAGA, is not a gathering of all of the US people but rather a political discourse and act on the whiteness of this country. For us it is a wakeup call for discernment to struggle. Yes, we belong, but as a daily act of resistance. Thus, to know ourselves is to know the brown reasoning of ourselves, the circulation of our sources and the ways in which we inhabit the borderland. Gloria Anzaldua has given us our itinerary, our territory and our spirituality: borderlands a *spiritual Mestizaje*.[9]

Aim at Changing Feelings too, not Only Ideas

The white reason has impinged on us a "codified madness" so we lose our forms of thinking and resistance. "Race" says Mbembe,

> is a form of primal representation. Unable to distinguish between the outside and the inside, between envelopes and their contents, it sends us, above all, back to surface simulacra. Taken to its limit, race becomes a perverse complex, a generator of fears and torments, of disturbed thoughts and terror, but especially of infinite sufferings and, ultimately, catastrophe. In its phantasmagoric dimensions, it is a sign of neurosis—phobic, obsessive, at times hysterical. As Frantz Fanon has noted, "race" is also the name for bitter resentment and the irrepressible desire for vengeance. "Race" is the name for the rage of those who, constrained by subjection, suffer injuries, all manner of violations and humiliations, and bear countless wounds."[10]

Under the MAGA "generator of fears and torments and thoughts of terror," we are seeing the infinite sorrows of our people, the catastrophe of our countries, and the merciless account on the lives of the immigrants,

---

9. In contrast to the notion that Anzaldúa maps a particular journey applicable only to other individual journeys, this shift from individual to collective perspective indicates that this critical mobility ideally enjoins others in its processes and perhaps achieves greater force through this intensification. It also practically recognizes that the transformations it enacts or foresees might exceed the individual frame, creating necessary collectivities. Her discussion here challenges exclusionary paradigms of nation, ethnicity, race, gender, and sexuality with the very terms that appear to authorize them, signaling a project of renewal that also requires resignification. Delgadillo, *Spiritual Mestizaje*, 224–28.

10. Mbembe, *Critique of Black Reason*, 385–91.

here and elsewhere. We must ponder the ways in which we have to deal with the emotional results of this madness, the ways in which we are drenched into paradoxical relations between feelings and actions, syndromes and disconnections, spiritual injuries, mental illnesses and resentments. How do we access these orbits and convolutions of emotional difficulties when we are the very ones who conjure psychological work as unnecessary and waste of time? As rage is a respondent to all of these calamities, we must muster our own selves, go deep into our own hearts and learn how to deal with it. So, our first movement is towards our soul so we find ways to keep the devouring mouth of rage to destroy us. Once we can understand that and deal with it, we can channel the energy of rage into forms of resistance and transformation and create paths of liberation.

Stay Connected to the Ground

Our ancestors were deeply connected to the earth, they knew their deep relations were done with the ground on which they lived, the animals around them, the waters, the fish, the birds, the seeds, the sky. Our modern life doesn't allow us to stop and connect with anything. Many of us are always running with projects and deadlines. Many are just trying to survive, just one step away from being completely rolled over by this economic situation. In whatever way, we must learn to pause, sit next to a tree and hear what the tree can tell us. As Job instruct us: "ask the animals, and they will teach you; the birds of the air, and they will tell you; ask the plants of the earth, and they will teach you; and the fish of the sea will declare to you."[11] We need to change our whole theological edifice and start from the ground, finding ways to deeply connect with the earth, gain our wisdom form the bio-system and those who have dealt with it for a while. Against the hydro-agri-business system of extractivism. What is the point of fighting for a world that is about to cease? We need to expand the notion of Martin Luther's King's beloved community and understand a community with the human and non-human and in a form of life together that does not entail the exclusion of anyone.

Knowing Our People

Our people rise, our people resist and protest. In the most wonderful ways. Our history is filled with moments in history when our people rose and

11. Job 12:7–8, NRSV.

created new worlds. They are resistance everywhere! Subcomandante Marcos and the Zapatista Army of National Liberation in Mexico is resisting! The Teachers Movement also in Mexico is resisting! The Landless Movement in Brazil resisting! The Argentina's Anti-Austerity Movement and the women are resisting! The students in Nicaragua are resisting! The campesino movement in Colombia is resisting! The environmental movement in Honduras is resisting! The queer movements everywhere are resisting! The indigenous communities everywhere are resisting!

And we also resist according to specific challenges with lots of fun. Let me tell you one story. Do you remember when lawyer Aaron Schlossberg shamed a staff person at a Manhattan eatery?" He shouted something like: My guess is they're not documented, so my next call is to ICE to have each one of them kicked out of my country. If they have the balls to come here and live off my money—I pay for their welfare. I pay for their ability to be here. The least they can do—the least they can do—is speak English.[12] All stupidities he said . . . Surely he called for a reaction. What happened in the next days is that "the city came out with several apt responses, one of which was a street party outside his flat—a protest in true Latino form. Lots of people went to the front of his apartment and brought a Mariachi band, tacos trucks, Pinatas with his face and loudspeakers playing reggaeton and Latin pop, with flags of all Hispanic countries. It was a fantastic party![13] We have to know our people well. We are blessed to be part of this fantastic group of people!

Creating an Aesthetics of Life and Death, Tears and Joy

At, under and around the wall, we laugh! We laugh hard! We laugh in time and out of time. We laugh in place and especially out of place. We defy death with our stubborn laughter. We laugh during the day and cry when night comes. We laugh and cry together. When there is the news of a son that was fund alive in the desert, when somebody goes to a detention center, when someone has crossed the desert safe, when someone is raped. We laugh and cry without ceasing!

The borders and the economic crushing of our communities are maddening. So, to find life out of this maddening process we must laugh and we must continue to do theologies as a network of support and sustenance

12. Wang, "'My next call is to ICE.'"
13. Magness, "He ranted at Spanish speakers."

11

to our people. God is fundamental to our people and we have this gift and this demand to help our people, with our people, to create knowledge, discourses and practices of faith that will defy the maddening and destruction of our communities. So, our theological work is unique.

Our theological work is filled with ambiguities and contradictions. But we don't shy away from it! We don't try to even it out or cut the edges so we can create a good proper European theology. Our theologies are broken, nonsensical, ridiculous, outrageous. Half sophisticated, half old fashion. Half written, half spoken. Half conscious, half unconscious. Half clear, half obscure. Half tears, half laughter. Half discourse, half songs. Half academic, half something else, whatever the fuck we want! We do what we want! Don't tell us what to do or not to do. We know it! The problem is that the academy might not consider it proper because we live in the midst of a magical realism. So, go figure us out! *Usted estan todos despistados.*

In our theologies, we decolonize the content, the format, the procedures, and the establishment of theological and religious thinking. We dress the way we want and we continue to be scholars. We call on different voices and nobody knows. We draw *maps for the feast*[14] that the gringos read *y se preguntan: Estan locos estes cucarachas? Que estan haciendo?*

They don't know that our laughter is like the redeeming power of God in Jesus Christ! Jesus Christ himself a laughter out of place. We are also homo ridiculous! That kind of ridiculous way of living/thinking that troubles the status quo. We console by laughing and admonish by crying. Our accent is our resistance, our smiling faces our gentle dismissal. We are a ball of incongruences and complexities because our lives are incongruent to this white system of thinking; our complexity comes from a mixture of people, sources, images and practices.

Tears and joys compose the main sources of the Latinxs communities. We preach and pray when we write our theologies and when do theology when we pray and preach. Our ears are attached to the ground, and our people matter more than our ideas. We see our people's brutal suffering; we see the thin line of our social fabric being destroyed faster than ever. We are at the edge of despair every single day. We hang on a thin rope over the abyss. Nonetheless, our tortillas and tamales, our singing and our fiestas will keep us going. As a Mexican avuela used to say: *Satanas quieres que desaparescas!* But we won't! We will take our place in this world and continue! For we carry the *esperanza transgressora* de Oscar Romero. We carry

14. Maduro, *Maps for a Fiesta.*

and produce theologies that pulse life in the midst of death, that mark and show the ambivalences of life and death from our people's main structures of life; namely, a life lived within utter necessities and demanding hopes, continuing disasters and ongoing faith, tears and pain, but also joyful songs of alegria. As the poet Geraldo Eustáquio de Souza said:

> Giving up . . . I've seriously thought about it but never really took myself seriously,
>
> I have more ground in my eyes than the fatigue in my legs,
>
> more hope in my footsteps, than sadness on my shoulders,
>
> more road in my heart than fear in my head.[15]

Living for us is a practice of resurrection! For we are seeds! Keep finding people and communities and places where your seed can resurrect! Find the reservoirs of life and give water to your people. Bring matter to what matters. Bring to life what does not matter. Speak beyond positivistic structures, speak and write in ways that go beyond the object/subject relation.

Concluding...

We now must come back to the words of Jesus.

"You see all these buildings, these policies, this brutality, this empire, do you not?

Truly I tell you, not one stone will be left here upon another; all will be thrown down.'

Meanwhile, 'Beware that no one leads you astray. Do not give up! Don't fall into desperation! Because "this is but the beginning of the birth pangs." This is just the end.

'Then they will hand our familias over to be tortured and will put them and you to death

Many will fall away, because they didn't stick together.

Instead they will betray one another and hate one another because they will fight over who is suffering the most while the poor ones will be killed.

And many false prophets will arise and lead many astray.

And because of the increase of lawlessness, the love of many will grow cold.

But anyone who endures to the end will be saved. "

15. Eustáquio de Souza, "Geraldo Eustáquio de Souza" (my translation).

The endurance that saves is the one that has all its trust in God. The endurance that saves is the endurance that pauses, that gets to know oneself and give attention to our interiors. The endurance that saves faces the daily threats to take away the lives of our people and keep the struggle! By the power of Holy Spirit! Endurance that knows how to sustain a combination of deep breaths, narratives and actions that are able to resist and counter the unruly, irresponsible, vitriolic and viciously violent use of the state machine of our time. The endurance that saves offers sobering courage to rise every mourning and go where people are placed on the cross!

The endurance that saves offers holy anger every afternoon and in a Fanonian way, "demanding human behavior from the other" and the end of unnecessary human suffering. The endurance that saves offers fierce love that resurrects us every evening, fierce love that helps to recollect ourselves so we can make a vigil with the most vulnerable. The endurance that saves stays at the borderland no matter what!

So, go out and get yourself even more committed to the poor, the undocumented, the immigrants and the refugees, join organizations that are working for change on the ground. If you go there, at the border, you will see that the challenges are way too intense and immense and the paradoxes insurmountable. And that it will keep us all very humble! Truly loving our people! And also, fired up so we can endure these times! And keep madness at bay.

May God bless us.

2

Why I'm Here

—MIGUEL A. DE LA TORRE

José was a simple man who worked with his calloused hands. He built things, trying to make a living as a carpenter; but times were hard, and taxes were high. In spite of the foreign military occupation of his homeland, there simply was no time to become involved with any of those revolutionary groups doing maneuvers and hiding in the wilderness. He kept his head down and worked hard, barely keeping food on the table for his rapidly growing family. Although a newlywed for a couple of months, his wife María already gave birth to a child that wasn't his, a healthy boy. On this particular night, José was scared. He ran through the sleeping town, silently making his way toward his makeshift home, praying and hoping he wasn't too late. He had to save his family from certain death! He burst into his shack going straight to the sleeping mats on the dirt floor. "*Despierta mi amor*, wake up my love," José told his wife as he gently shook her. "A messenger just warned me *la milicia*, the militia, will be coming for us. I fear we will disappear! *Apúrate*, hurry up, we must leave this moment for a safer land, far from the reaches of this brutal dictatorship." There was no time to pack any belongings or personal mementoes, nor was there time to bid farewell to friends and family. In the middle of the night, literally a few steps before the National Guard, José took his small family into *el exilio*, the exile. They would come to a foreign country, wearing only the clothes on their backs. Even though they could not speak the language, nor understand the

15

idiosyncrasies of the dominant culture, at least they were physically safe. Salvation for this poor family was found *south* of the border.[1]

Over two millenniums ago this family arrived in Egypt as political refugees, fleeing the tyrannical regime of Herod. Almost fifty-seven years ago my own father came home to his wife, my mother, with similar news. Because of his involvement with the former political regime, he was now marked for death by the newly installed government. If caught, he would surely face a firing squad. They gathered me, their six-month-old child, and headed north, arriving in this country literally with only the clothes on their backs. Like Jesús, I too was a child political refugee

The story of God's people is the story of aliens. The stories of Abraham, Isaac, Jacob, and Joseph are the stories of aliens attempting to survive among a people not their own in a land they cannot claim. If they were living today, we would probably call them undocumented immigrants, or the more pejorative term: "illegal". The people who came to be called Jews, are a people formed in the foreign land of Egypt. They become a nation while traversing the desert, having no land to claim as their own. They experienced exile in a far-off place called Babylon and disenfranchisement on their own terrain due to colonial military occupation by a foreign empire, Rome.

Throughout the biblical text we are reminded of God's concern for the alien and the stranger who resides among us. Aliens and strangers in the Bible are those who have been victimized, oppressed, or enslaved by others; those who are vulnerable because they lack family connections or support; and those whose nationality or religion differs from the dominant culture. In the exodus story, God told the Israelites to welcome the stranger because "you were once aliens in the land of Egypt." Ruth, a Moabite woman "clings to" her mother-in-law Naomi to provide her security in old age even though she could have returned to her own people. The Good Samaritan in Luke does not leave the alien on the side of the road, nor builds walls to avoid seeing his injuries; he takes social and economic risks to attend to the alien's needs.

According to biblical scholar Leticia Guardiola-Sáenz, "Jesús live[s] between borders, in a hybrid space which is an experience similar to that of Hispanics/Latin Americans in the postcolonial and neocolonial era. [Jesús], *the border-crosser*, the traveler between cities and villages, between heaven and earth, between suffering and bliss, comes to redeem the border-crosser who refuses to conform to the limits and borders of a

1. De La Torre, *Reading the Bible from the Margins*, 112–13.

16

society that has ignored her voice, her body and the borders of her identity as Other."[2] Most border-crossers today act out of desperation; Jesús, theologically speaking, acted out of solidarity with the least of these. The biblical text reminds us that although divine, Jesús became human, assuming the condition of the alienated (Ph. 2:6–8). The incarnation's radicalness is not that the Creator of the universe became human, but rather God chose to become poor, specifically a wandering migrant. This reveals a Jesús who assumes the role of the ultra-disenfranchised. Because God incarnated Godself among the marginalized, Jesús connotes a political ethics lost on those accustomed to the privilege of citizenship within the empire, missing the significance of Jesús the "illegal."

Did Jesús cry himself to sleep as I did? Feeling the same shame of inferiority imposed by the dominant culture? Did he have to become the family translator, as I did, between a dominant culture who looked down with distain at parents not fluent in the *lingua franca*, witnessing a role reversal of having to learn from children about the wider world? And of course, the shame felt by the child-translator toward those parents for appearing less-than the dominant culture who masters the language; and yet simultaneously, the tremendous fear and burden of knowing a mistranslation can lead to precarious situations as some within the dominant culture seek an opportunity to defraud the migrants. For some of us who have been the intermediates between the dominant culture and our families, discover in Jesús a savior, a liberator who knows our anxieties and frustrations. But why was Jesús physically present in Egypt? While a link between the Jesús crossing the border into Egypt, and the Jesús crossing the border into the United States exists; I rather explore why Jesús crossed borders in the first place. To answer this question is to answer why I too crossed borders. Why am I here?

On June 21, 1960, I received the government's affidavit—a toddler, too young to understand the letter's importance. At the time my parents and I were living in a roach- and rat-infested one-room apartment in the slums of New York City, sharing one bathroom with the other tenants on the floor. Two months earlier, we arrived in this country with a tourist visa. The letter, citing Section 242 of the Immigration and Nationality Act, notified me deportation procedures were imminent; and I should therefore "self deport" in lieu of forced expatriation. Ironically, I found myself in the country

2. Guardiola-Sáenz, "Border-crossing and Its Redemptive Power in John 7:53—8:11," 151.

17

directly responsible for my original exile from my homeland. Truthfully, I would have preferred to stay and live in my own country, among my own people, rooted in my own culture. And yet, when this life comes to an end, my bones will be interned in this foreign soil, a land which never fully embraced me, regardless of the decades of contributing to its welfare. So why am I here? Why do I reside in what my intellectual mentor, José Martí called "the belly of the beast"? Contrary to popular mythology, we did not come seeking liberty or pursuing economic opportunities; we came because of sugar, rum, and tobacco (the three necessities of life). We are in this alien land as a direct result of U.S. foreign policies designed to deprive my country of origin, Cuba, of political and economic sovereignty during the first half of the twentieth century.

The reason I—and many of my fellow Latinxs—are here is a paradox conveniently ignored by politicians and absent from the current immigration debate. Rather than wrestling with the causes of immigration from south of the border, we instead batter around red herrings like anchor babies, the taking away jobs from real Americans, or seeking to unfairly use up generous social services provided by taxpayers. Or, more politically correct, we come in search of the American Dream, hoping for a better life for our families. Unfortunately, these narratives are all erroneous. We are forced to leave our homelands for the insecurity of border crossing because the United States empire—like all colonizers—created political and economic uncertainty in our countries of origins due to a foreign policy designed to secure the avarice of multinational corporations.

In an unapologetic attempt to garner votes, right-wing politicians rile against illegals, presenting the undocumented as a threat to U.S. security and a danger to everyday "real" Americans. Donald Trump best illustrates this with his campaign announcement speech where he refers to Mexicans as "bringing drugs. . . bringing crime. . . [and being] rapists."[3] Unfortunately, this type of bigoted anti-immigrant rhetoric is the norm of a current neo-nativist attitude. During the 2016 presidential elections, Republican candidates—speaking to their base—engaged in a one-upmanship of outdoing their opponents by proposing greater life-threatening intolerance to the cheers of approving crowds. All advocate weaponized drones targeting border-crossers, constructing a 2,000-mile fence stretching from the

3. Michelle Ye Hee Lee, "Donald Trump's False Comments," *Washington Post.* https://www.washingtonpost.com/news/fact-checker/wp/2015/07/08/donald-trumps-false-comments-connecting-mexican-immigrants-and-crime/?noredirect=on

Pacific to the Gulf, and building more private prisons to accompany the entire family (including babies and children).

We should not be surprised that conservative-leaning politicians are hostile to Latinx immigration. But rather than rehash their blatant racism, I will instead focus on the problematic rhetoric normatively expressed by liberals who engage in the rhetoric of hospitality. During the 2016 democratic presidential primary debate, Martin O'Malley approached immigration by stating, "We are not a country that should send children away and send them back to certain death." He called "hospitality to strangers" an "essential human dignity."[4] Who could argue against hospitality? After all, this virtue becomes a religious and civic duty to assist (bring salvation) to these poor unfortunate souls. It's what Jesus would do. Hospitality is a biblical concept meaning more than just opening one's home to the stranger and inviting them for a meal. The Hebrew Bible God consistently reminds us to remember Abram the alien, or the Hebrews' time in Egypt as slaves; and thus, offer justice to the sojourner residing in our midst. The New Testament God reminds us how some who showed hospitality to strangers, entertained angels without realizing (Heb 13:2). The biblical terms "stranger" or "sojourner" captures the predicament of the today's U.S. undocumented immigrant from Mexico or Central America. The term connotes the in-between space of neither being native-born nor a foreigner. As such, the alien lacks the benefits and protection ordinarily provided to those tied to land due to their birthplace. Vulnerable to those who profit from their labor, aliens derive security from the biblical mandate of hospitality. Alien's treatment is based on three biblical presuppositions: 1) the Jews were once aliens who were oppressed by the natives of the land of Egypt (Exod 22:21); 2) God always sides and intervenes to liberate the disenfranchised (Exod 23:9); and 3) God's covenant with Israel is contingent on all members of the community benefitting, regardless if they are Jewish or not (Deut 26:11).

The importance of the New Testament passage of José and his family seeking refuge in Egypt, is often lost on those with the privilege of citizenship. Yet for those who are or have been undocumented, they read in these verses a God actively connecting with the hopelessness of being uprooted. Responsibility toward aliens is so paramount, God incarnated God's self as an alien fleeing the oppressive consequences of the empire of the time. Herod's responsibility was to ensure profits, in the form of taxes, flowed to the Roman center with as little resistance as possible. Obviously, he also benefited

4. Hing, "Who Would Win an Immigration Debate."

financially, as do many Latin American elites today who sign trade agreements destructive to their compatriots. To ask why Jesús, a colonized man, was in Egypt is to ask why Latinxs today are in the United States.

Colonization during the time of Jesús brought about a push factor where his family, out of fear for their lives, fled toward Egypt; just as it pushed my own family northward due to the same reasons. The economic, political, and foreign policies of the United States caused this push factor in Latin America, specifically Central America, as people either lose their farms and livelihoods or fled in fear of the governments established in their countries through the might of Washington. Simultaneously, in the quest for cheap labor within the U.S., a pull factor is also created. Crossing the border, described as a festering scar caused by the First World rubbing against the Third, becomes a life-threatening venture. The U.S. has a Latin American immigration problem because for the past two hundred years, its wealth was based on stealing the cheap labor and natural resources of its neighboring countries.

As Rome benefited by *pax romana*[5] brought about by territorial expansion, North Americans benefitted by *pax americana*, known throughout the nineteenth century by its jingoist religious ideological term "Manifest Destiny,"[6] which justified Anglo territorial expansion. Acquiring land had more to do than with simply divine inspiration. With the new possessions came all the gold deposits in California, copper deposits in Arizona and New Mexico, silver deposits in Nevada, oil in Texas, and all of the natural harbors (except Veracruz) necessary for commerce along the California coast. By ignoring the provisions of the peace treaty signed with Mexico; the U.S. government was able to dismiss the historic land titles Mexicans held, allowing white U.S. citizens to obtain the natural resources embedded in the land. These natural resources, along with cheap Mexican labor fueled the U.S. industrial revolution allowing overall U.S. economy to develop and

---

5. Latin for "the Roman peace"

6. John L. O'Sullivan is credited with coining the term "Manifest Destiny" in his 1839 newspaper essay, "The Great Nation of Futurity." By synthesizing a romanticized ideal of nationalism with the economic ideology of unlimited progress, O'Sullivan ushered in a national myth which impacted American politics from 1840 to the early 1900s. Anglo-Saxons were believed to be destined by God to settle the entire North American continent; called to develop its natural resources and spreading liberty, democracy, and Protestantism. Besides justifying westward expansionism, Manifest Destiny's racial overtones influenced the conquest and removal of indigenous people from their lands. Today Manifest Destiny is understood to be the ideology behind U.S. colonialism and imperialism.

function, while economically dooming Mexico by preventing the nation from capitalizing on its stolen natural resources.

We must consider the nineteenth century policy of Manifest Destiny. This pseudo-religious ideology believed God gave whites a new promised land encompassing the entire Western Hemisphere. Perhaps the staunchest supporter was James K. Polk, eleventh president, who while on the campaign trail promised to annex Texas and engage Mexico in war if elected. Once taking office, he deployed troops into Mexican territory to solicit the desired response of having the Mexican army first fire upon the invading U.S. army. The Mexican–American War ended with Mexico's capitulation, ceding half her territory. A surveyor line was drawn across the sand upon an area which, according to the archeological evidence, has historically experienced fluid migration. This expansionist war against Mexico was minimized by the false creation of the U.S.'s historical meganarrative designed to mask the fact it was the empire who crossed the borders—not the other way around.

We must also consider how the twentieth century policy of "gunboat diplomacy"[7] unleashed a colonial venture depriving Central American countries of their natural resources while providing the U.S. with an unlimited supply of cheap labor. President Theodore Roosevelt laid the foundation for the enrichment of today's multinational corporations. Roosevelt's foreign policy placed the full force of the U.S. military, specifically the marines, at the disposal of U.S. corporations, specifically the United Fruit Company, to protect their business interest. Nicknamed "*El Pulpo*"—the Octopus—because its tentacles extended into every power structure within Central America, the United Fruit Company was able to set prices, taxes, and employee treatment free from local government intervention. By 1930, the company had a sixty-three percent share of the banana market. Any nation in "our" Hemisphere which attempted to claim their sovereignty to the detriment of U.S. business interests could expect the U.S. to invade and set up a new government (hence the term "banana republic"—coined in 1935 to describe servile dictatorships). It is no coincidence the rise of U.S. banana consumption coincided with the

7. Gunboat diplomacy, like big stick diplomacy, refers to the U.S. pursuit of foreign policy objectives through the display of military might, specifically through the use of naval power in the Caribbean basin. This normative 20th century U.S. international policy constituted a direct threat of violence and warfare toward any nation who would choose to pursue its own sovereign destiny by refusing to agree to the terms imposed by the superior imperial force.

rise of U.S. imperialist actions throughout the Caribbean Basin. During the twentieth century, the U.S. invaded at least twenty-one countries and participated in at least twenty-six CIA led covert operations throughout the Caribbean basin to institute regime change, even when some of those countries, like Guatemala had democratically elected governments.

More important than territorial expansion during the nineteenth century, was the U.S. hegemonic attempt to control economies of other nations during the twentieth century. While empires of old, like Rome, relied on brute force, the U.S. Empire instead relies on economic force—not to disregard the fact it also has the largest military apparatus ever known to humanity. Through its economic might, the United States dictates terms of trade with other nations, guaranteeing benefits continue to flow northward toward the center and the elites from the countries who signed the trade agreements. Consider the consequences of implementing the 1994 North American Free Trade Agreement (NAFTA) which destroyed the Mexican agricultural sector. Dumping U.S. surplus corn on Mexico (about $4 billion a year during the first decade of NAFTA)[8] meant a 70% drop in Mexican maize prices, while housing, food, and other living essentials increased by 247%.[9] In the first ten years of NAFTA, at least 1.3 million Mexican maize farmers lost their small plots of land unable to compete with cheaper U.S. subsidized corn.[10] When Mexican farmers were squeezed out due to their inability to compete with U.S. subsidized corn, U.S.-owned transnational traders, like Cargill and Maseca, were able to step in and monopolize the corn sector through speculating on trading trends. They used their power within the market to manipulate movements on biofuel demand and thus artificially inflate the price of corn many times over.[11] Worsening the plight of the maize campesino were the structural adjustments imposed on Mexico by the World Bank in 1991, eliminating all government price supports and subsidies for corn.[12]

8. Barrionuevo, "Mountains of Corn."

9. López, *Farmworkers' Journal*, 7–9, 41.

10. Labor Council for Latin American Advancement (LCLAA), *Another America Is Possible: The Impact of NAFTA on the U.S. Latino Community and Lessons for Future Trade Agreements*, Product ID 9013 (Washington, DC: Public Citizen's Global Trade Watch, 2004), 4–8.

11. Bello, "World Bank, the IMF, and the Multinationals." See also Barrionuevo, "Mountains of Corn."

12. López, *Farmworkers' Journal*, 7–9, 41.

These sufferers of neoliberalism are Jesús in the here and now. God chooses the oppressed of history—the hungry, the thirsty, the naked, the alien, the sick, the prisoner—and makes them the cornerstone, the principal means for salvation for the world. In fact, whatsoever we do to these, the very least among us—we do it unto Jesús. And because the undocumented crossing the borders are usually the hungry, the thirsty, the naked, and of course the alien; because they are often the sick due to the hazards of their journey, and when caught by the Border Patrol become the prisoner; if we want to see the face of Jesús, we just need to gaze into the face of the undocumented. God does not appear to the Pharaohs or Caesars or Prime Ministers or Presidents of history; for leaders of empires whose policies cause death and migration are more aligned with the satanic than with the divine. God appears as and to their slaves, their vassals, and those alienated by their empires.

The undocumented attempt the hazardous crossing because our foreign and trade policies from the nineteenth through the twentieth-first century have created an economic situation in their countries where they are unable to feed their families. When one country build roads into another country to extract, by brute force if necessary, their natural resources; why should we be surprised when the inhabitants of those same countries, myself included, take those same roads following all that has been stolen. I am in the United States because I am following my stolen resources: my sugar, my tobacco, and my rum. To ignore the consequences of colonialism leads to the virtue of hospitality. For many from the dominant culture with more liberal understanding of the biblical text, hospitality undergirds how they approach and treat the undocumented. While it may always be desirable for all to participate in this virtue, caution is required least the practice of hospitality masks deep-rooted injustices. This virtue of hospitality, I argue, is not the best way to approach our current immigration crises.

The U.S. has an immigration crisis, yet a failure exists in recognizing the reason we come is because we are following what has been stolen from us. We come to escape the violence and terror the U.S. historically unleashed upon us in an effort to protect *pax americana*, a needed status quo if American foreign business interests are to flourish. An immigration problem exists because, for over a century and a half, the U.S. has exploited—and continues to exploit via NAFTA—their neighbors to the south.

To read the Jesús narrative through white eyes is to respond to the immigration moral crises by advocating hospitality. But hospitality assumes ownership of the house where Christian charity compels sharing one's possession. To read the biblical narrative of Jesús from the perspective of the undocumented alien is to argue Latin American cheap labor and natural resources are responsible for building the house. My sugar, my rum, and my tobacco built it, and I want my damn house back. Due to U.S. sponsored "banana republics" throughout the nineteenth and twentieth century; Latin Americans holds a lien on this U.S. house's title. Rather than speaking about the virtue of hospitality, it would historically be more accurate to speak about the responsibility of restitution.[13] Maybe the ethical question we should therefore be asking is not "why" are they coming, why I am here; but, how does U.S. begin to make reparations for all that has been stolen to create the present economic empire? The Jesús biblical narrative forces us to ask: What does the U.S. colonial Empire owe Latin America for all it has stolen?

13. De La Torre, *Trails of Hope and Terror*, 9–14.

3

"Being White These Days"[1]

—Robert P. Hoch

"Being white these days is not what it used to be."[2]
—Nell I. Painter

For years, I've been intrigued by something that I experienced on the Camino de Santiago in Spain: while the way goes through beautiful rolling hills, the pilgrim path also passes through the hearts of major cities, with all the "harms and charms" of an urban setting. And at times, on that urban road, you sojourn with people who are not on the road in any temporary sense, but for whom the road is life. I vividly remember the experience of visiting with people who were homeless as we, the "official" *pelegrinos*, walked the Camino. At first, I thought they were *pelegrinos* just like us: tattered, browned by the sun, looking not so different from the ground beneath their feet, our feet. The differences between us *almost* vanished, like a border almost vanishes, but not quite.

That experience leads me to ask how our journey as white preachers forms us, especially given the topic of this collection of essays, preaching in/on the border. Conceived of as a journey, do we, as white preachers, stay in our lane? Or do we break from the conventional, approved pathways, as an act of the will? Or is that even possible? Have borders vanished? Or do

---

1. Dedicated to my dear friend and colleague in ministry, The Reverend Doctor Henry E. Fawcett, June 24, 1932 to May 11, 2019. Until we meet again . . .

2. Painter, *History of White People*, 389, quoted in Alcoff, *Future of Whiteness*, 1.

we exaggerate, at our peril, the existence of a post-racial world, freed from such boundary markers? Are borders fixed or do they move?

Today, this morning, I talked with an African American on our street, a predominantly white, upper middle-class neighborhood. He wore a patch over one eye. His name, I learned, was Moses. A Hebrew in *Pharaoh's* neighborhood; it wasn't *his* neighborhood. If we had met in his neighborhood, which was down past Eutaw, towards Sandtown-Winchester, where the Freddy Grey uprising of 2016 got its start, we might not have spoken at all. More than likely, we would not have met because, on the rare occasions that I am in that community, I don't often get out of the car, at least not alone. When I do, it has a social action component, alongside other churches and grass-roots organizations, often responding to yet another act of gun violence. But, on this day, Moses was passing through where I live, a migrant in my neighborhood. He was hungry. I was not. He was on foot. I was driving a car. He was picking up something I had left on the street, for anyone who wanted it.

Moses was the body of anyone black.

My body . . . was the body of anyone white.

In a preaching seminar, an African American pastor asked me, "What does it mean to you that you're a white preacher in a black city?" I immediately stiffened against the question. My reaction was physical, bodily rather than theoretical. Irrespective, it was a fair question, both in terms of my body and Baltimore's demographic make-up. Baltimore has been majority-African American for well-over two decades. Inhabiting this white body, what does it mean for me to preach in a historically white church where the borders of whiteness are narrower than they used to be, but not vanished?

As for my body, it's difficult to say what being white means. Being white means different things. I am white in skin and I am Alaska Native by descent. The latter supplies a meaningful explanation for my lived experience. Yet, given the way white people talk about race, i.e. check the box, or in terms of fractions, my experience is lost in translation. But that's not the only reason it's difficult to talk about. I remember how my great aunts (you would consider them full-blooded by appearance), stood around my white great-grandfather's grave in Fairbanks: one was so angry, she wouldn't come near it; the other stood near the grave, his power to terrorize seemingly remote. But they were agreed on one thing. Impatient with my persistent questions, they demanded, "Why do you want to know about the past? The past is unhappy. Leave it!"

Maybe that's what it means to be a white preacher in this black city . . . or at least part of what it means.

Growing up, we were rural poor, but not urban poor, which seems to me far harder (certainly riskier) than anything I ever experienced. Baltimore has pockets of wealth and pockets that look like war zones. The church I serve is known as progressive and inclusive; we are not as white as we used to be. We're not as hetero as we once were. As a minister, I walk into a pulpit that has ties to the first president of the United States, George Washington. I also join walks where I've stood on the corner, sometimes in the exact place, where people have been shot dead, or mortally wounded, including children.

My son goes to a charter school in the city of Baltimore. His classmates ask him why his eyes are blue. My daughters go to a private school; its campus reminds me of Princeton University. No one asks about their blue eyes.

Borders seem fixed. But they're not fixed and perhaps they never were. Indeed, not only do we move, but the borders shift as well. In other words, many people are happy to be tourists, including me. Being a tourist is such an enriching, horizon-expanding experience. And you get to fly home. But becoming a pilgrim, which is closer to the root identity of a migrant, requires something else again, something like dishevelment of body and spirit or it is initiated by what philosopher Linda Martín Alcoff, author *The Future of Whiteness*, calls a "new-found incoherence."[3]

In my contribution to this work, I'm going to talk more about whiteness than I have in the past. Maybe it's a reckoning of sorts, with the white man in the grave, the one my aunts wanted me to forget, fear, or flee, and the man I am in the mirror. I may need to remember him for reasons larger than my own but not less than my own.

As for the reasons larger than my own in 2016, I returned to parish ministry in Baltimore. As a result, I am more sharply attuned than I have been in the past to the sense that those who preach do so in contexts of multiple and complex crises. Agnes W. Norfleet, pastor of the Brynn Mawr Presbyterian Church in Bryn Mawr, PA, writes that "[p]reaching in the age of Trump is no picnic." She goes on to say what many of us in the pulpit have felt:

> These three decades have seen the multiple crises of rising urban homelessness and rural poverty, wars and rumors of wars,

---

3. Alcoff, *Future of Whiteness*, 170.

terrorist attacks, earthquakes, tsunamis and hurricanes, famine across continents, migrations of refugees, escalating gun violence, the frightening degradation of the environment, and the increasingly voluminous #MeToo movement. *Through all these critical moments and developments is woven a tangled and insidious web of racism.*[4]

In the face of these multiple crises, she pleas for something at once different and yet also surprising from my perspective as a long-time theological educator in one of the Presbyterian Church (USA) seminaries:

> Those of us seasoned preachers who have gained a fair measure of expertise for interpreting scripture, consulting biblical scholarship and theological resources in order to relate texts to the world around us, need a different kind of help now. We need more guidance exegeting current movements and social institutions in order to figure out what is happening in a rapidly changing cultural and political milieu.[5]

I argue that pulpit interpretations of scripture and the theological tradition have been ill-served by the ostensibly anti-racist essentialism of left-wing, liberal and inclusive white congregations. Alcoff argues that there are both racist and antiracist notions of white exceptionalism, which she says is synonymous with white essentialism.[6] While the most obvious forms of white terrorism are located in right-wing communities, the understandings of whiteness that prevail in both conservative and liberal churches (antiracist) are in in effect essentialist accounts of whiteness. It is the one color that is beyond all others or it is against all others, but, in either case, it is exceptional. Against this, Alcoff insists that, "there is no exceptionalism about whiteness."[7] Essentialist approaches to whiteness (even when they promote antiracist views) do an end run around the difficult, messy, uncomfortable task of race-talk in white America. Worse, they short-circuit any possibility of rearticulating whiteness for a less racist future.

4. Norfleet, "One New Book for the Preacher," 45.

5. Norfleet, "One New Book" in *Journal for Preachers*, 45.

6. Alcoff, *Future of Whiteness*, 101.

7. Alcoff, *Future of Whiteness*, 29.

Coherent Theology

> "Before he allegedly walked into a synagogue in Poway, Calif., and opened fire, John Earnest appears to have *written* . . ."

That's the way the reporter introduces the manifesto, which was written by the alleged white terrorist, Jeremy Earnest, in the religion section of *The Washington Post*. He wrote . . . and what he appears to have written was *theological*. According to the accounts of what happened, Earnest walked into the Chabad Synagogue on the last day of Passover in Poway, California, where he opened fire. Unsurprisingly, Earnest's manifesto "spewed" racist ideas about Jews and other racial groups. It also included what pastors saw as "cogent Christian theology." Ironically, what shocked anti-racist pastors was not the racist ideas, which they rejected out-of-hand as incompatible with their system of belief, but the familiarity of his theology: "Several pastors said they found the manifesto's parts about salvation significantly more troubling [than they did its grievances against Jewish people]. Because when it came to what it said about salvation, they *agreed* with it" (my emphasis). Said one Presbyterian Church in America pastor, "[Y]ou actually hear a frighteningly clear articulation of Christian theology in certain sentences and paragraphs. He has, in some ways, been well taught in the church." Rev. Mika Edmondson, pastor in the Orthodox Presbyterian Church (where Earnest and his family regularly attended) said this: "It certainly calls for a good amount of soul-searching. We can't pretend as though we didn't have some responsibility for him—he was radicalized into white nationalism from within the very midst of our church."[8]

While the article does not indicate the specific make-up of Edmondson's congregation, it does cite Pew Research that indicates that 81% of those who are evangelical Presbyterian are white and, presumably, capable of generating theologically coherent statements. Perhaps, in light of what has happened, the statements aren't as coherent as they initially sounded. Along these lines, one pastor explained the act of terror as a form of mental illness, isolated to this individual. No one seriously disputes that this was mental illness, but perhaps it was a peculiar form of white mental illness. Maybe, in the absence of honest talk, delusional talk was the only race-talk going. At the level of subjective whiteness, children like Earnest "are

---

8. Zauzmer, "Alleged Synagogue Shooter was a Churchgoer who Talked Christian Theology."

systematically taught to become delusional."[9] Quoting from W.E.B. Du Bois, the manifesto isn't an anomalous form of "mental illness"; racist acts of violence "are not instances of 'Europe gone mad' but of Europe itself, 'the real soul of white culture . . . stripped and visible today.'"[10]

The rest of my work here will reflect on obstacles to talk about whiteness, including theological problems; the genre of the "unglorious white" narrative as it helps us to see and experience whiteness as contingent and lived rather than fixed and abstract; and concludes with a brief reflection on the path of preaching.

Obstacles to Talk about Whiteness

Reading the reactions of Edmondson, it feels as if theology were, in effect, playing in a post-racial world but the world isn't post-racial, at least not in a social sense. In the midst of a majority white church, race-talk was either absent or infrequent and yet it was as obvious as the bodies present and the bodies absent on a Sunday morning, the most infamously segregated hour in America. Perhaps whiteness was seen as, at best, extraneous or, at worst, an ideological "add on" to biblical and theological interpretation.

And it was not talked about, at least not in any depth. Why? Martin Alcoff believes that it is not only an ideological discomfort but an actual reflexive reaction to the lingering feeling of white shame around the Civil Rights struggle. In a white liberal congregation, even broaching the question of whether cultural appropriation is taking place when a white soloist sings an African American spiritual generates physical reactions. What is the source of that "stiffening" of white resistance? Alcoff quotes Bob Dylan's partner at the time, Suze Rotolo, who locates this discomfort with media coverage during the Civil Rights period: "'Pure unadulterated white racism was splattered all over the media as the violence against civil rights workers escalated. White people were looking at themselves and what their history had wrought, like a domestic animal having its face shoved into its own urine.'"[11] Feelings of shame translate into avoidance and awkwardness.

A second obstacle to realistic talk about whiteness is demographic in nature. Much of the anti-racist movement up until recently has been

9. Alcoff, *Future of Whiteness*, 84.

10. DuBois, *Souls of White Folk* in W.E.B. Du Bois, ed., *Writings*, quoted in Alcoff, *Future of Whiteness*, 140.

11. Alcoff, *Future of Whiteness*, 14–15.

premised on whites being in the majority. In this position, whites can set the terms of negotiation. Those days are quickly coming to an end, according to the U.S. Census Bureau. Census predictions say that the white majority will cease to exist by the year 2050. "Whites will have to jockey for position in a multi-polar nation . . ."[12]

The third obstacle to naming whiteness in America exists when we believe that we are now or nearly post-racial. She points to theoretical attempts to get around race as forms of "eliminativism", a term she coins to name theories that "eliminate" whiteness as a meaningful category of social description. Eliminativist theories on the left, she will say, can be grouped into three main camps. The first is that race is pure social construction. Constructions are imposed from the top down. We should live fully-consciousness of the falsehood of racial construction. The 1999 film, *The Matrix*, suggests this particular view: its heroes exist and act in the matrix, a digitally produced illusion, but they act as pure traitors. Neo and Trinity exert unique and apparently super-powered volitional control over the "false construction" of reality. It's cool but ultimately useless and worse as a social theory of whiteness. Alcoff counters that our social identities refer to something real, empirically measurable, and not constructed. This leads to the second family of eliminativist approaches to race, which is to say the whole category of race is too problematic. Science has demonstrated that race is not a biological phenomenon but instead a social one. However, having noted the absence of a biological source for racial identity does not render that category meaningless. Human beings live in social worlds and not merely biologically determined ones. The third camp is represented by those who believe that whiteness is on its way out. The boundaries, they will say, are crumbling and with it, categories of race, including especially whiteness. Alcoff believes that, indeed, the lived experience of whiteness is changing but it is not realistic to imagine that it is going to disappear soon. A social theory of whiteness can only be useful so long as it predicts the continuation of whiteness, at least for the time being.[13]

Each of these anti-racist positions is founded on a version of American essentialism. To the point, she asserts that the doctrine of American Exceptionalism, the idea that American history represents a decisive break with histories of the "old world", is nothing more than white exceptionalism posing,

12. Alcoff, *Future of Whiteness*, 3.
13. Alcoff, *Future of Whiteness*, 148–49.

or passing, as a nonracial theory."[14] We must name and claim whiteness as a realistic social category, rather than a mythologized (white supremacy) or constructed category (liberal progressive). Whiteness is real, it is racist, and it is subject to rearticulation. It is not that she takes a neutral position, far from it. "What whiteness explains," she writes, "is racial oppression."[15] But that isn't "all it is" and certainly cannot be if it is to form a part of a "less racist future."[16] To that end, she proposes a social realist analytic as a tool for testing the explanatory truthfulness of our social identities.

In order to move the conversation forward, she proposes a four-part social realist analytic for race as a social phenomenon. Each part of this analytic constitutes a "small theory" for explaining our social identities. They are small and thus, by definition, susceptible to scrutiny and revision.[17] First, the way we experience ourselves has **explanatory power**. It helps us organize our reactions to others or their reaction to us. Second, social identities are **material practices**. We can actually see or hear the physical or sensory qualities of our social identities.[18] Third, social identities contribute to what Alcoff refers to as **social attunement** or what we notice or foreground as important and what we push into the background, as unimportant, suggests our social identity as well. "Our sensitivity to slight often varies by group identity, leading to charges of "oversensitivity" by those who do not share those perceptual attunements."[19] Social identities correlate our immersion into "systems of collective meaning" with a communal organization. Fourth, social categories of identity arise from **historical experiences**. Many of our identities arise from a group-related historical event. Another way of looking at this thread of our social identity is that it conveys "'history's gravity'" to our social narratives, as they reinforce "congealed distrust" and "deep rules" which in turn organize our perception of our relationships between different groups.[20]

Alcoff's small theories of social identity foster a more complex, more empirical, more nuanced, and more helpful account of the social phenomenon of race than the eliminative approaches summarized above. Taken

14. Alcoff, *Future of Whiteness*, 103.
15. Alcoff, *Future of Whiteness*, 96.
16. Alcoff, *Future of Whiteness*, 97.
17. Alcoff, *Future of Whiteness*, 47–8.
18. Alcoff, *Future of Whiteness*, 49.
19. Alcoff, *Future of Whiteness*, 52.
20. Alcoff, *Future of Whiteness*, 55.

together, we get what Hans George Gadamer calls the "horizon of meaning"—that horizon helps us to recognize our particular attunements. It also disabuses us of the notion that our social identity is an act of the will.

How is whiteness different from other social identities? It cannot be the "same" as being black or Latino in America. A thing called white terrorism exists, even though it is often not named as such. So also does the notion that whiteness is the "vanguard" of civilization, science, literature, wisdom. Categories of empirical whiteness (the ability of social scientists to predict behavior, income differentials, education, schools), imaginary whiteness (myths, for example, of Columbus "discovering" American), and subjective whiteness (the notion that there is a white way of being in the world) all inform or shape a unique and "disanalogous" notion of whiteness relative to other racial-ethnic communities.[21] These she says make a persuasive case that whiteness is in some way essentially and irretrievably bound to racism. In the end, however, she concludes that, while useful, whiteness without contingency is effectively whiteness beyond salvage and it is also incoherent because it lacks context: "The bottom line . . . is that meanings are determined by use, either overt or covert ones, and use is always specific to context. And contexts change."[22] With this relatively straight-forward argument, Alcoff shifts the discussion in a more helpful direction, in which the salvage of a less racist future, including the rearticulation of whiteness, becomes possible. It is not that whiteness, as a social phenomenon, is not racist, but only that racism is not all that it is. People who undergo experiences of "new found incoherence" may be capacitated for a transformation.

Unglorious White Narratives

Alcoff believes a social realist analytic can equip us to narrate the "unglorious white narrative"—such narratives, she would say, eschew idealism, prefer ambiguity, and acknowledge internal contradiction. Especially striking in this regard is the story of C. P. Ellis, one-time Grand Cyclops of the KKK. He grew up, poor white and had absorbed deep feelings of shame and inferiority. One day, the KKK invited him to attend a meeting. No one had invited him to anything in his whole life. Ellis joined. He rose through the ranks. He was an organizer. He organized terror, but still he organized. And in his own words,

21. Alcoff, *Future of Whiteness*, 74–90.
22. Alcoff, *Future of Whiteness*, 117.

he said, "I felt very big." Looking back, he said he had never felt so affirmed, so important as when he belonged to the Klan.

When integration came, he was not only big, he was useful, especially to middle class white people, who were fighting integration. But something happened one day to make him think that maybe he was just being used. He was still racist, but somehow the lie got to him. Meanwhile, he'd been approached by a person who had been charged with integrating the schools. Since he was a leader in the Klan, and had connections in the white power structure, he was tagged as someone who might be instrumental in organizing the support of the white constituencies. To do so, the organizer said he would need to work with a Black woman, Ann Atwater, who was also known to use violence in her commitment to civil rights.

Ellis could not imagine working with a black woman, forget eating with her. But when he got the sense that he was being used by people who would never actually share his hope for his children, something snapped. Or something was set free. He saw her sitting alone, following a meeting. And he walked over. Things were weighing on him. He sat down next to her and they started talking. He had children and she did, too.

And he said what they knew, that when integration happened, the middle- and upper-class whites would move their kids to the private schools. And the economic base of the public schools would evaporate. As he talked, he started to cry. She touched him gently. Alcoff would probably say that a kind of "identity incoherence" was conceived in that moment of empathy and common concern. It got to him.

He went to the Klan with all the zeal of a convert. His erstwhile friends weren't hearing it. He was turned out and, suddenly, unemployed. Eventually, he got work as a machinist at Duke University. He was the only white man on a unionist team. He was elected to chief machinist by his peers. He continued to stay in touch with Atwater. When he died, she came to his funeral. She came in early, sat down in the front pew. An usher saw her and walked up to her. From just behind she heard him clear his throat: "Excuse me," he said, "this service is a private service."

"I know," she said.

Pause. "It's for family only."

"Yes, I know," she replied, irritated. "C.P. is my brother."[23]

23. Adapted from Alcoff, *Future of Whiteness*, 196–203.

Unpacking this vignette, Alcoff cites what she calls the role played by victims, whose positioning gives them a capacity to see the world through the eyes of others who share similar hopes (education and economic prosperity) but also because the narratives of the principles and powers fail to fully explain their experience of vulnerability, their capacity for transformation, and their instinct for out-of-bounds creativity. C.P. Ellis represents a type of intersectional activist who acts as a human being who is also white. Martín Alcoff concludes:

> The solution [for a less racist future of whiteness] will not be found in a flaccid universal humanism, nor in a pursuit of white redemption, nor in a call to a race-transcendent vision of class struggle. Rather the solution will be found in facing the truths about who we are, how we got here, and then developing an offensive strategy for achieving a future in which we all can find a place.[24]

Perhaps this also includes a hermeneutics of pastoral offense for those who preach.

Difficult Preaching: Rearticulating Whiteness

Alcoff's analytic exposes racially neutral narratives as non-racial theory masking a white essentialism. Racially neutral narratives place whiteness beyond the rainbow. Our task, according to Alcoff, is to return whiteness to the rainbow; or, as a pastoral theologian might say, return whiteness to the rainbow, part and parcel of the diversity of God's creation. We do so, in part, by introducing race-talk that will inevitably make majority white churches uncomfortable. That is better than leaving whiteness unstated in the anti-racist church while white supremacists, Christian and otherwise, talk about race with deadly consequences.

Alcoff notes that just broaching the issue creates anxiety among her white students and then, playfully, she suggests that we talk about it in the safe space of a book. A sermon is both safe and terrifying at the same time. We will need to name feelings of shame, fear, as well as firmly debunking ideals of a post-racial universe and we will need to do that in church, in the Sunday morning sermon. By naming the peculiarity of, say, how a white soloist sings an African American spiritual, we open ourselves to some uncomfortable acts of exposure: is a white soloist

---

24. Alcoff, *Future of Whiteness*, 204.

singing an African American spiritual a respectable form of white liberal "black-face"? What do people of color think or feel when they witness the "nearly" perfect execution of an African American spiritual by a white soloist? Does that feeling rise to the level of deliberate reflection, in the context of alliances that sometimes exist between people who, for one reason or another, share a common interest?

As for white people themselves, examples or exemplars, do we attune our interpretive antenna to non-typical stories of whiteness, which suggest realism as well as hope? How will we know that what we are dealing with is an unglorious white narrative? Or how might we name the "glorious white narrative" or call out the sentimental narrative, which loops back into false ideas about whiteness, e.g. the *Driving Miss Daisy* variety?

About six months ago, a story about a young African American man from Baltimore and a white man from western Maryland made the local news. It was forwarded to me by a nationally recognized journalist who worships at our church in Baltimore. When I read it, I felt conflicted. Why? It was a story about a white person, from western Maryland, who, after being diagnosed with a heart malady, began a long wait for a transplant at the Johns Hopkins Hospital in East Baltimore, an area known for its urban violence. As it happened, their lives were joined together when the young man was shot in the face, the bullet lodging in his brain. The young black man was taken to the hospital, a few floors below the white man, who was waiting for a heart transplant. The young man's mother looked at the scanner indicating brain activity and said it was like the screen after the cable goes off. It wasn't hard, she said, to tell the doctors to take him off life support. But what came after was hard: the heart of her young African American son was transplanted into the body of a white man in his mid-fifties.

This story should offend us. It shouldn't be easy. The dangers of such a story are legion, including trading on sentimental readings of that narrative. But the social locations and lived experiences of each person are important, as well as acknowledging our own "stiffening" against this story, which is in part a reaction of shame to the raw violence of white supremacy in Baltimore. Lived narratives, however, exist irrespective of our shame and, as those who preach, naming those "incoherent" narratives are urgently important. In this story, a relationship was formed, initiated by the organ transplant recipient. It was a complicated relationship, to be sure. The reporter closes with a tender story of how, when they first met in the Johns Hopkins Hospital, the man asked her to "listen" to her son's heart. "It's beating fast today," he said. The writer, however, closes the story with a sharp note of realism, as if to staunch the easy denouement of white privilege: "With tears running down her face, she listened to the beating heart of her dead son."[25]

As preachers, how do we tap into the unglorious white narrative? This may almost be impossible. Risks are inevitable; but plain talk is necessary, messy talk is urgently required. We're not going to get it right. Maybe that is as it should be. Yet this modicum of humility exists in tension with the thoughtful analyses of whiteness which, in effect, give us an instrument for the evaluation and testing of white experience. This sort of scholarship begins to answer Norfleet's plea for "more guidance" on contemporary social movements. Many of us, speaking now as a pastor, have inherited the boiler-plate language of apologetic whiteness. We quote MLK Jr., we apologize for crimes against humanity; or we step gingerly around the landmines of talk about reparations for fear of the messiness that will inevitably ensue. Alcoff, and writers like her, supply a realistic and yet hopeful analytic of whiteness. We can gain much by a close study of works like hers; the careful integration of their social analyses into our hermeneutical approaches to the sermon can capacitate us for more realistic rearticulation of whiteness in our preaching lives.

However, there are at least two other elephants in this room. One is the theological tradition itself: many view race-talk as intrinsically antithetical to Christ talk. This was borne out for me in a recent conversation with an acquaintance who was puzzled by my insistence that we engage in talk about whiteness in the church: "But once we become Christian, none of that really matters, does it?" Her reaction sounds strangely bland, not at all gripping or startling, as one might expect from an experience of the alternative world of Jesus Christ. Indeed, the response reflects an essentialist view of theology, a story that ignores what is social and politically obvious, as obvious as a Jewish man dying on a Roman cross or white terrorism by way of a lynching tree in South Carolina.

Dietrich Bonhoeffer's meditation on the "natural world" suggests a theological way of thinking about race talk in the pulpit. The created order, he says, has fallen and we live in the natural world. The natural world exists towards the new creation even as it continues to struggle with the fallen world. Typically, preachers get this, as for instance, where emotional suffering is concerned: preachers do not fly (one hopes) to the new

25. Prudente, "Two Men, One Heart."

PREACHING IN/AND THE BORDERLANDS

creation, with happy sermons on Revelation where there are neither tears, nor suffering, nor pain anymore. But with race, we may be less comfortable, particularly when the question is not race in general but whiteness in particular. We want to "skip" to the perfect unity promised in Christ. If we don't skip, we may find that to preach in this key is prophetic, but it also has a pastoral note, insofar that it gives a diagnosis of a corporate sin peculiar to white people in North America. Acknowledging shame, both explicitly and subtly, plays an important role in releasing white people from their captivity to idealistic notions of whiteness.

In his diagnosis of the German setting, Bonhoeffer notes that ideologies level everything. Finding natural, lived ways to talk about whiteness and its relationship to others cuts against the grain. According to Bonhoeffer, Christ destroys the posturing of the heroic being with being humans loved by God:

> Christian people do not form the world with their ideas. Rather, Christ forms human beings to a form the same as Christ's own. However, just as the form of Christ is misperceived where he is understood essentially as the teacher of a pious and good life, so formation of human beings is also wrongly understood where one sees it only as guidance for a pious and good life. . . To be conformed to the one who has become human—that is what being human really means. The human being should and may be human. All super-humanity . . . fall away from a person here . . . because they are untrue. *The real human being is the object neither of contempt nor of deification, but the object of the love of God.*[26]

Finding authentic, not-quite-perfect narratives of whiteness in the throes of rearticulation is crucial; our capacity to detect such narratives may arise not from our ideas but rather Christ's being human.

Paul's declaration in Galatians that there is neither Jew nor Gentile is, in many ways, the get-out-of race talk for Christians. And yet, in tension with that, we find ample evidence of the early church grappling with the way the Spirit upended borders, but not completely, so that the agents in the story were startled or confused. The natural world might be a way of naming, for instance, the way the narrator of Acts depicts a heightened (and realistic) consciousness about the borders of race, gender, and ethnicity that narratives of unacknowledged whiteness may be ill-equipped to name. For instance, think specifically of the story of Peter and Cornelius, which is

26. Bonhoeffer, *Ethics*, 93–94 (my italics).

ostensibly a story about Cornelius' conversion but, on closer examination, reveals a double conversion and perhaps, by implication, a kind of double consciousness (Acts 10:1–33). And later, when Peter returns to Jerusalem, is it something analogous to W.E.B. DuBois' double-consciousness which we see in Peter's "step-by-step" explanation of why he was eating and drinking in the house of a gentile? Peter does not go on to "catechize" Cornelius but returns to Jerusalem to catechize Jewish Christians in a "repentance that leads to life" (Acts 11:1–18).

Hermeneutically, interpreters might naturally, out of habit, identify with Peter. However, if read with a socially realistic lens about whiteness, the interpreter might recognize an analogical connection between Cornelius and American whiteness: Cornelius, while generous and sympathetic for Jewish Christians, was nevertheless a Roman centurion. Does he return to the Roman garrison, as Peter did to the church in Jerusalem, with the message that he belongs to a crucified Jew, whom he also calls Christ and Lord? We don't know, but we can ask what that might look like. What are the obstacles to that kind conversation/conversion? In other words, as happens with the Ethiopian eunuch, the narrator leaves unresolved how the "convert" negotiates her or his new identity in the "old world" in which borders were set and immoveable.

Ambiguity of that sort is not accidental in scripture; it prompts our pastoral imagination, allowing us to interrogate how the borders of whiteness shift as a result of our confession of a crucified Jew as Christ and Lord. The Spirit supplies the impetus for these movements, so that neither Jew nor Gentile, male nor female, slave nor free enjoys perfect coherence. The sense that Cornelius is confused (he imagines that Peter must be a god) and Peter is genuinely perplexed ("Why have you sent for me?") is one of the first indications that something new is emerging, that boundaries of identity have been shifted in some profound way.

The other elephant in the room is the "invisible" white preacher. I remember the first time I preached on white terrorism in America. It was in 1996, during the burnings of black churches throughout the south. The church where I was serving had preached, prayed, and potlucked happily through that season of fires before I realized, to my horror, that we hadn't even offered a prayer of intercession for the black communities that were being terrorized all around us. When we did respond, the session (the governing body of our local congregation) almost scuttled any action over a dispute about whether these fires were set by the members of the church (so they could collect insurance) or the KKK. This was a conservative congregation which would have described itself as anti-racist. In the end, the church pledged to help rebuild the destroyed church which was about 30–minutes from my church's location. Yet the leaders in the church deliberately set to one side the uncomfortable conversation about whiteness in order to maintain the "invisible" quality white goodness. I was a part of that conspiracy.

It's a long time since I stood with my aunts near my great-grandfather's grave, their father. In preaching, I find that there is something in me that flees that person as well as something that is almost clinical in its assessment of my relationship to him. My spouse saw a picture of me once in which she said I looked like my great-grandfather. That resemblance upset me. Looking back, I suppose my aunts saw that resemblance, too. I was a young man by then, probably old enough to have developed some of the features of the man they knew and feared as their father. I carry something of him whenever I enter the pulpit. Whiteness is, inevitably, more complicated than it seems. It's not comfortable being complicated. But it might be the way forward for us all, naming our lived experiences, as honestly and simply as we can.

4

Making U.S. Protestant Disciples of All Nations

—Gerald C. Liu

A Historical Protestant Bias in U.S. History

As we discuss "Preaching in/and the Borderlands" in contemporary U.S. culture, it is vital to recognize that preaching has enunciated and helped establish an elemental Protestant bias within the history of U.S. foreign policy and immigration. Here, Protestantism describes a multiplicity of denominations including Baptists, Congregationalists, Episcopalians, Lutherans, Disciples of Christ, Methodists, Presbyterians, and others not formally affiliated with Catholic or Orthodox traditions of Christianity. Religious and ethical zeal for and from Protestantism was foundational to establishing a de facto empire of liberty abroad. Religious liberty associated with a Protestant outlook preceded the championing of human rights. It ordered the welcome of immigrants into American life domestically. It continues to inform and trouble the ways in which we square human diversity, American citizenship, and the aims of American democracy today.

On November 25, 1848, at the 18th Street Methodist Episcopal Church in New York, the Reverend Abiathar M. Osbon preached a sermon titled, "The duty of America to her immigrant citizens" from Lev 19:33–34: "And if a stranger sojourn with thee in your land, ye shall not vex him. But the stranger that dwelleth with you shall be unto you as one born among you, and thou shalt love him as thyself; for ye were strangers in the land of Egypt: I am the Lord your God" (KJV).[1] By "immigrant citizens," Osbon did not principally have in mind foreign born populations from Latin America, Asia, Africa, or the Middle East, as some might have today. Rather, he addressed American fears regarding "Roman Catholicity" and "Romanism." He implored, "Is it not true, to a criminal extent, that the term *foreigner* is one of reproach among us, and that of Catholic even a term of opprobrium?"[2] Yet he exhorted his listeners to see the "Irishman," "Frenchman," "Swede," and "Spaniard" as sharing the history that "God made of one flesh all men to dwell upon the face of the earth."[3] Osbon assured his listeners that eventually, with the right kind of democratic hospitality and opportunities for social mobility and freedom, Catholic immigrants would see that America is not only a Christian nation, but a Protestant one to which they could belong. He made it clear precisely what kind of Christianity would unify America's newly immigrated. It wasn't Catholicism. "Nay," Osbon retorted, "Protestantism is the religion of America."[4] Driving home the point further and expanding it beyond the Catholics whom he presumably saw as clear candidates for Protestant conversion, he also asked his listeners, "What are we? Are we Pagans? Are we Mohammedans? Are we Jews? Are we Papists? You know we are not."[5] Although Osbon's zeal might sound strange to us today, his sermon named a foundational and pervasive historical bias for Protestantism within American religious identity. His words were not only prejudiced, but also prophetic.

They captured how American Protestantism would grow into a gospel of religious liberty crucial to expanding the nation's global influence and power. In 1898, half of a century after Osbon's sermon, the United States won a ten-week battle known as the Spanish-American War. The war effectively disbanded the Spanish Empire, a Catholic regime, with no American casualties. The U.S. intervened to aid with Cuban independence, and through strategic military deployments, the signing of the Treaty of Paris in December of 1898, and the transfer of $20 million as part of treaty negotiations, the U.S. ended up taking control of Spanish colonies, including Puerto Rico, Guam, and the Philippines. By January of 1899, as Reinaldo L.

1. Osbon, "The duty of America to her immigrant citizens."
2. Osbon, "The Duty of America to Her Immigrant Citizens," 18.
3. Osbon, "The Duty of America to Her Immigrant Citizens."
4. Osbon, "The Duty of America to Her Immigrant Citizens," 25.
5. Osbon, "The Duty of America to Her Immigrant Citizens."

Román notes in *Governing Spirits: Religion, Miracles and Spectacles in Cuba and Puerto Rico*, the *Boletín Eclesiástico* of Puerto Rico, a Catholic Diocesan journal, reported the merging of twenty of the eighty-seven Catholic parishes and a nearly thirty percent decrease in the number of priests in Puerto Rico overall.[6] More than thirty-six priests left for Spain after the American occupation. The mergers and decline of clergy coincided with a sense that Puerto Rico was breaking with its Spanish and Catholic past (though Catholicism remained vibrant through the leadership of committed laity in the absence of ordained clergy), and moving into a future of adopted democracy marked by the legislation of religious freedom and clearer separation between church and state, democratic ideals with Protestant roots.[7]

After witnessing a spate of failed governorships and seeing the critical need for stability in Guam because of its maritime and naval significance, President McKinley commissioned Richard Leary, a Navy admiral, as Naval Governor of Guam in 1899. Leary's opening remarks to the people of Guam declared, "All political rights heretofore exercized [sic] by the Clergy in dominating the people of the Island, are hereby abolished, and everyone is guaranteed absolute freedom of worship and full protection in the lawful pursuits of life, as long as that protection is deserved by actual submission to and compliance with the requirements of the Government of the United States."[8] Leary was a salty and stern leader, who, according to historian Robert Rogers, angered American Catholics when he noted that he had "disposed the priests who were the ringleaders in encouraging vicious and demoralizing habits and customs" in a progress report to his commanders.[9] Purging Catholic leadership and fracturing the possibility of future ecclesiastical governance by instituting the Protestant ideal of religious liberty proved crucial in bringing the American version of democratic stability to Guam.

6 Román, *Governing Spirits*, 53; see also 221nn7 and 8. For more on the role of American Protestantism and anti-Catholicism influencing governance of Puerto Rico, see Ayala and Bernabe, *Puerto Rico in the American Century*, 16ff.

7. For a deeper study into how Protestant ideals such as freedom of conscience coincided with the constitutional amendment of religious freedom and its subsequent applications in domestic and global American policy, see Feldman, *Please Don't Wish Me a Merry Christmas: A Critical History of the Separation of Church and State*. Feldman writes, "Protestant reformers long had equated the free exercise of religion with freedom of conscience. The framers' [of the Constitution] generation was no different (166)."

8 Rogers, *Destiny's Landfall*, 111.

9 Rogers, *Destiny's Landfall*, 113.

The islands of the Philippines would not become states and no clear economic or military rationale justified their annexation. Yet the U.S. government took interest in them as a gateway to China and as a stretch of land for growing ideological projects. As Anna Su writes in *Exporting Freedom: Religious Liberty and American Power,* "The Philippines provided an opportunity to see the spirit of humanitarianism prevalent in the late nineteenth century in action, one more site of the moral reform movements of American Protestants."[10] To the U.S., the Filipinos were incapable of self-rule due to the limitations of their race. The Catholic heritage of the islands was thought to be defective and the conditions seemed ideal to introduce Protestant liberty and save the Filipinos from themselves.

According to *The Christian Advocate,* a Methodist Episcopal weekly that had become one of the largest circulating weeklies in the United States with more than 30,000 subscribers and 150,000 readers by the 1830s. On November 21, 1899, it reported that President William McKinley, also a lifelong Methodist, announced at a meeting with the General Missionary Committee of the Methodist Episcopal Church, "Hold a moment longer! Not quite yet, gentlemen! Before you go, I would like to say just a word about the Philippine business." McKinley then admitted that while the islands "came to us, as a gift from the gods, I did not know what to do with them." Apparently, consultations with Democrats and Republicans proved to be unhelpful as McKinley himself stated, "I sought counsel from all sides—Democrats as well as Republicans—but got little help." McKinley would need divine intervention.

After nights spent pacing and thinking, McKinley told the pastors, "I went down on my knees and prayed Almighty God for light and guidance" until it finally came to him one evening:

> there was nothing left for us to do but to take them all, and to educate the Filipinos, and uplift and civilize and Christianize them, and by God's grace do the very best we could by them, as our fellow-men for whom Christ also died. And then I went to bed, and went to sleep, and slept soundly, and the next morning I sent for the chief engineer of the War Department (our mapmaker), and I told him to put the Philippines on the map of the United States (pointing to a large map on the wall of his office), and there they are and there they will stay while I am President![11]

10 Su, *Exporting Freedom,* 14–15.

11. Rusling, "Interview with President William McKinley," 17. See also "Manifest Destiny, Continued: President McKinley Defends U.S. Expansionism."

For McKinley and his successor Theodore Roosevelt, Christianizing the Filipinos meant establishing religious freedom while removing Filipino political independence and altering the Filipino religious landscape with two clever acts of diplomacy that will be retold in microform.

First, land disputes with the former Catholic regime, known as the friar lands controversy, were settled with a $7 million purchase from an American Philippines commission. Through this purchase, Spanish friars would not relinquish ownership of thousands of acres of the best Filipino agricultural lands and the U.S. would not take the lands by force. Rather, negotiations with the Vatican were held according to the protections of the Treaty of Paris. The U.S. guaranteed the protection of land ownership so that the friars could sell the lands at a self-regulated pace. With the new ownership and the departure of the Spanish friars came space for American clergy to serve as replacements and assist in the establishment of an autonomous Philippine Church. This reconfiguration redefined Filipino Christian religiosity according to U.S. notions of religious liberty. For example, the rite of marriage shifted according to American mandates from a strictly ecclesiastical solemnization to a civil institution.[12]

Second, the U.S. avoided further conflict and ensured religious freedom on the islands by brokering with the Moro population, Muslim inhabitants of the southern Philippine islands and provinces, in order to replace their Islamic law courts with secular ones. The sultan's religious leadership would remain intact, but his political authority would not. The U.S. levied a poll tax and prohibited Islamic provisions for slavery and polygamy. In another move to liberalize the Moros, the U.S. granted the right of private land ownership to them. While providing freedom of religion, a political ideal based upon the Protestant hegemony within American culture at the time, the U.S. policies altered the practices of Islam in the Philippines and subjugated them to American ideals of progress and civilization.[13]

At home, the United States maintained a separation of church and state. Yet in the Philippines, Christianity, especially as informed by Protestantism and democratic ambitions, morphed into a diplomacy of religious liberty that enabled the U.S. to reconcile the American conscience with the nation's imperialist ascent, according to Su. Protestant idealism morphed into domestic and global statecraft. And, more broadly, reflecting the sermon from Reverend Osbon a few decades earlier, Christian

12 Su, *Exporting Freedom,* 27–28.

13 Su, *Exporting Freedom,* 33–34.

Protestantism shaped the actions of domestic and foreign affairs just as the nation began to grow into its role as a global superpower and destination for emigrants from across the world.

The entry of the United States into World War I and the subsequent victory in that military campaign provided a transnational stage for promoting U.S. foreign policy as determined by Protestantism and its related iterations. As the minister for The First Church of Christ in Hartford, Connecticut, Rockwell Harmon Potter preached a Thanksgiving Day sermon, saying, "[T]he dominant motive which led our nation to war was *the Christian motive of good will for all men, the Christian motive of love for humanity*."[14] For Potter, the theological providence of the First World War was revealed through the peace it brought, a peace for which we ought to give thanks. At the same time, this peace was "not the peace of an absence of fighting," but "of a concord of peoples, the peace that issues from the will of God, progressively wrought into the structure of the international life, into the fabric of the world."[15] In Potter's view, "the Kingdom of God cannot be won until it is won together."[16] By expounding upon a peace "issu[ing] from the will of God," "wrought into the structure of the international life," and "into the fabric of the world," Potter's sermon models the ways in which a Protestant outlook weaves seamlessly to inform and construct a political hopefulness in the burgeoning status of the U.S. as a global superpower.

Yet even as the United States secured its worldwide dominance following the Second World War, exercising the "proprietary relationship" between Protestantism and the United States as a nation lost its wattage. It came under suspicion, especially at home.[17] The nation began to diversify at a rapid pace and Christianity had less of a foothold in the national conscience than it did in previous generations with the ascent of American multiculturalism. In response to this diversification, Evangelicals sought to protect the idea of a "Christian America" and entrenched themselves in organizations like the National Association of Evangelicals, going as far as campaigning for an amendment to the Constitution that would include a reference to Jesus of Nazareth and his God in both 1947 and 1954. Mainline Protestants, including the Methodists, American Baptists, Congregationalists, Presbyterians,

---

14 Potter, "Meaning of Victory and Peace." Italics original.

15. Potter, "Meaning of Victory and Peace."

16. Potter, "Meaning of Victory and Peace.

17. Hollinger, *After Cloven Tongues of Fire.*

Lutherans, and Episcopalians, began to self-interrogate their previous aims and identify new avenues for wider social change.

They balanced worry over the waning interest in church by taking up moral issues in the public realm. David Hollinger points out that in 1961, the Lutheran historian Martin Marty wondered if the inauguration of Catholic President John F. Kennedy marked "the end of Protestantism as a national religion and its advent as the distinctive faith of a creative minority."[18] Three years later, the Episcopal layman William Stringfellow wrote an excoriating critique of racism toward African Americans after living in impoverished Harlem, entitled, *My People is the Enemy: An Autobiographical Polemic*. And, as liberal or ecumenical Protestants (as Hollinger calls them) renounced their earlier "sexist, imperialist, homophobic, unscientific and excessively nationalistic" pronouncements and approaches to ministry and the Civil Rights Act (1964), the Voting Rights Act (1965), and the National Immigration and Nationality Act (1965) each passed, the latter finally overturned the 1882 Chinese Exclusion Act in full, recalculated immigration quotas from all countries, and eliminated immigration restrictions for family members and immigrants with "special" status. Yet, the real numbers of attendance in American Protestant churches showed loss in members in absolute numbers.[19] And so, what was lost in the pews was offset by gains in the public sphere as Mainline Protestant values began to influence legislation.

The Enduring Legacy of Protestant Hegemony

Though Protestant hegemony wanes, it still persists in U.S. policy with respect to policy regarding diplomatic power abroad and immigration policy at home. Consider the evolution in ecumenical Protestantism from a bigoted past to a continuous moral force, both rectifying social inequities and promoting human rights from the mid-twentieth century onward. On the one hand, the transformation could be seen as an improvement in the overt prejudice articulated by sermons like Osbon's and theocratic triumphalism transmitted in messages like Potter's. On the other hand, it can also be read as a repositioning of ecumenical Protestantism as a normative lens for negotiating borderlands at home and abroad. In *Religious Difference in a Secular Age: A Minority Report,* the late cultural anthropologist Saba Mahmood writes

18. Hollinger, *After Cloven Tongues of Fire*, 24.
19. Hollinger, *After Cloven Tongues of Fire*, 37.

about the ways in which the modern secular state has in fact exacerbated religious tensions in postcolonial Egypt.[20] By "secular state," Mahmood means a "globally shared form of political structuration" and she views religious liberty as foundational to that structure. Her interpretation of the modern secular state in Egypt provides a comparative touchpoint for understanding how the American political absorption and use of Protestant ideals, such as religious liberty, made the global spread of democracy accessible in territories like Puerto Rico, Guam, and the Philippines. Religious liberty can function both as foundation and vaulted ideal to reconfigure the political culture of nations whose sovereignty is lost even as democracy spreads. That reconfiguration, as seen in the aftermath of the Spanish-American War, involves the displacement and redistribution of religious leadership within territorialized contexts. And misshapen sermons often provided theological rationale to justify the political maneuvering and conquests of the U.S. as it built a modern empire without calling it one.

In a 2016 report, the Pew Research Center counted a record number of refugees relocating to the United States in the 2016 fiscal year. Of some 85,000 refugees reported, around forty-six percent of them were Muslim and about forty-four percent were Christian refugees.[21] The Cato Institute, tracking trend lines from the U.S. Department of State, reports that since the immigration policy executive order of the Trump administration, Muslim refugees have fallen ninety-one percent below their rate in the 2016 fiscal year. Sunni Muslim refugees have plummeted ninety-eight percent and Shi'ite Muslims eighty-six percent. While Trump has claimed to make Christian refugees a priority, even those numbers have fallen by sixty-three percent since 2016.[22] While more recent numbers are still being tabulated at the time of this writing, 2018 reported the fewest refugees admitted entry into the United States in forty years. President Donald Trump's recent insistence upon building a border wall, even at the expense of threatening the livelihood of government workers, his travel ban, the appointments of Mike Pompeo and John Bolton, and their ties with anti-Muslim authors and conspiracy theorists display clear prejudice at the highest levels of U.S. governance. All three politicians are Protestants—Trump and Pompeo are Presbyterians and Bolton is a Lutheran. Their Islamophobic political decisions suggest that one could reintroduce

20. Mahmood, *Religious Difference in a Secular Age.*

21. Connor, "U.S. admits record number of Muslim refugees in 2016."

22. Bier, "U.S. Approves Far Fewer Muslim Refugees, Immigrants, & Travelers."

Osbon's rhetorical homiletic question from nearly 170 years ago and wonder if those politicians view Islam as a kind of opprobrium. Trump has stated that "faith is more powerful than government. And nothing is more powerful than God."[23] Pompeo shared with a Wichita, Kansas, church group a more measured statement, "[i]t is absolutely a minority within the Muslim faith, but these folks are serious, and they abhor Christians, and will continue to press against us until we make sure that we pray and stand and fight and make sure that we know that Jesus Christ our Savior is truly the only solution for our world."[24] At an annual United Against Nuclear Iran summit, Bolton issued a warning to the "mullahs in Tehran": "If you cross us, our allies, or our partners; if you harm our citizens; if you continue to lie, cheat, and deceive, yes, there will indeed be hell to pay."[25] Identifying how much preaching has influenced their discriminatory political leadership exceeds the scope of the reflection here, but their words certainly sound like proclamations of political theology.

Instead, I will note the way in which these figures seem to have forgotten a distinct American innovative expression of Protestantism, namely religious liberty, and how it was marshalled to exercise imperial ambitions without the overt establishment of empire. By remembering the complicated, anti-Catholic, anti-Semitic, racist, xenophobic, and imperial past of Protestant hegemony and its relationship to domestic and global U.S. governance, Trump, Pompeo, and Bolton might consider whether they are misinterpreting Protestantism once again or distorting a positive interpretation of it for the sake of securing the political power of the United States, except this time, without much concern for the protection of others to believe and worship in peace. This is not to say that religious extremism should go unchecked.

I dined on a boardwalk with a friend in Dahab, Egypt on the evening of Orthodox Easter on April 23, 2006. The next night, during the celebration of Sharm El Nessim, a celebration marking the beginning of spring, the boardwalk was devastated by three nail bombs. We had departed that morning on a bus. In 2015, I ran with a friend to the finish line of the Boston Marathon an hour before pressure-cooker bombs tore through it. I currently live just over a half mile from where a truck driver killed pedestrians

23. Green, "Trump Creates a not-so-new Faith Office in the White House."

24 Michael W. Chapman, "CIA Dir. Pompeo: 'Jesus Christ Our Savior Is Truly the Only Solution For Our World.'"

25. TOI Staff and Agencies, "Bolton Warns Iran of 'Hell to Pay' in Impassioned NY Speech."

and bikers by running over them on the Hudson River Parkway. The day was Halloween or the eve of All Saints' Day. Of course, we must protect American citizens and prevent this kind of violence as much as we can, and the associations with distorted religious belief cannot be ignored. Yet as the nation wrestles with how to confront such evil, responding with force will not suffice. We must also develop more thorough understanding of our neighbors from other religious traditions and check the ways in which the United States has misinterpreted Protestantism and Christianity in general toward violent ends. The current essay has raised the example of McKinley's deliberations regarding the Philippines, but the misinterpretation of Christian belief has fueled far worse in terms of American political life. Take for example the depopulation of indigenous peoples and the use of Africans as slave labor, two national transgressions for which we still have not adequately atoned, and that were absolutely essential for the formation of what we now call the United States of America.

In the late Shahab Ahmed's 2016 AAR Best Book in the History of Religions, *What is Islam?: The Importance of Being Islamic,* Ahmed asserts that Islam is neither an object nor a categorization, nor is it a unified belief that is correct. Rather, Islam is an exploration of the meaningful marked by contradictions in theory and practice. As we think about the things that lie ahead in terms of preaching in/and the borderlands, perhaps we ought to ask whether the Protestant hegemony that has guided U.S. immigration policy and imperialism historically is now also in a similar milieu, one of wide contradictions in theory and practice. How can Christian preachers, who are eager and open to do the will of God at the borders, learn from the violent and checkered history of domestic and global American diplomacy driven by Protestant ideals like religious liberty? How might preachers investigate panoramic (and I believe, peace-oriented) scholarship like Ahmed's to become more effective proclaimers who nurture people of faith while not excluding followers of other faiths? How might preachers prevent illogical Christian conviction or an appetite for violence out of love for country and cultivate faith that lives into a truer expression of Jesus's words to love our neighbors as ourselves in Mark 12:31 and the command of Lev 19:33–34: "And if a stranger sojourn with thee in your land, ye shall not vex him. But the stranger that dwelleth with you shall be unto you as one born among you, and thou shalt love him as thyself; for ye were strangers in the land of Egypt: I am the Lord your God."? By attending to questions like these, we will utter new horizons of hope.

5

An Overview of the Current Landscape of Immigration Law

—Sarah Ellen Eads Adkins, JD

The Immigration and Nationality Act, the set of laws that governs immigrating to the United States, encompasses 8 books, roughly 500 pages each. That is to say, this short chapter will give you a very basic overview of the general types of immigrations statuses, a few of the more common ways people become lawful immigrants, and a brief description of what it means to be undocumented.[1]

Though immigration policies and trends have shifted since the beginning of the United States, the most relevant change to the modern immigration system occurred in 1965.[2] At the height of the civil rights movement, Congress passed and President Johnson signed a major

---

1. This chapter is intended to give you a very basic overview of immigration law; it is not meant to provide any type of legal advice in any circumstance whatsoever. If you have an immigration law question, you should speak to an attorney. The Catholic Legal Immigration Network maintains a list of nonprofit immigration clinics in every state: https://cliniclegal.org.

2. For a more comprehensive overview of the history of immigration law, beginning with exclusionist policies in the colonies prior to the Declaration of Independence, *see* Kozen and Götzke, *American Immigration Policy*, 123; and John Powell, *Immigration*, 3. For a comprehensive review of the politics behind immigration law in the United States, see Tichenor, *Dividing Lines*.

overhaul in the United States immigration system, the Immigration and Nationality Act of 1965.[3]

Prior to this Act, the United States' immigration laws were highly exclusionary, explicitly excluding immigrants from Asian countries with the Chinese Exclusion Act.[4] The Act of 1965 significantly increased the opportunity to immigrate through family preference categories.[5] This Act has had a profound impact on modern immigration law. In 1960, there were around nine million immigrants in the United states; by 1980, that number had increased to over fourteen million.[6] Further, the demographics of immigrants to the United States changed significantly. United States immigrants changed "from mostly European to mostly Asian and Hispanic."[7] Broadly speaking, "[i]mmigrants from Latin American benefited from the family unification provisions of the 1965 Act while Asian immigrants benefited from their possession of special occupational skills, abilities, or training."[8]

Currently, the percentage of immigrants in the United States population is at a near record high, at 13.5%, and 43.7 million immigrants in 2016.[9] This change is escalating rapidly; the Census has projected that America will become a "majority-minority" country in 2042, "meaning no single racial and ethnic group will comprise a majority."[10]

United States immigration law is a highly complicated area of law and each step and status listed in this chapter has an exception and each exception has an exception. But it is important to have a baseline knowledge of the different types of immigration statuses and the current state of immigration law because, without that knowledge, we cannot meaningfully preach or speak on immigration. If we do not understand the hurdles immigrants

---

3. Abramitzky, "Immigration in American Economic History." Interestingly, this bill was not seen as a major overhaul of the immigration system in its time. When announced by President Johnson, he said, "This bill that we will sign today is not a revolutionary bill. It does not affect the lives of millions. It will not reshape the structure of our daily lives, or really add importantly to either our wealth or our power." Johnson, "Remarks at Signing of the Immigration Bill."

4. USCIS History Office and Library, *Overview of INS History*, 3.

5. Abramitzky, "Immigration in American Economic History;" Tienda, "Multiplying Diversity."

6. Radford, "Facts on U.S. Immigrants, 2016."

7. Kozen and Götzke, *American Immigration Policy*, 12.

8. Kozen and Götzke, *American Immigration Policy*, 12.

9. López, "Key Findings About U.S. Immigrants."

10. Wong, *The Politics of Immigration*, 20.

face to come to the United States, we cannot understand why anyone would risk their family's lives walking across a desert to cross the border. If we do not understand what a lawful permanent resident is, we cannot meaningfully advocate that undocumented immigrants brought here as children against their own volition should obtain that status.

Immigration law changes constantly and is often at the forefront of American politics.[11] In the final month of preparing this chapter, the United States government has been shut down over whether or not to extend the current border wall to protect the southern border from unlawful migration.[12] This chapter is merely meant to give a broad overview of the most common types of immigration statuses and ways to immigrate to the United States, though the details will certainly change over time.

Citizens and Lawful Permanent Residents

Immigration is governed by three executive agencies: the State Department issues visas for those entering the United States; the Department of Labor regulates certain types of worker visas; and the Department for Homeland Security (DHS) administers nearly every other type of immigration application.[13] Within DHS, United States Citizenship and Immigration Services (USCIS) processes immigration applications and applications for naturalization; Immigration and Customs Enforcement (ICE) is the enforcement arm of DHS; and Customs and Border Patrol (CBP) protects international borders.[14]

The following overview will begin with how individuals become United States Citizens and will continue to explain the various visas that lead to permanent residency, starting with the most common and progressing through the least common types of visas.

---

11. Because immigration law shifts so quickly, the United States Citizenship and Immigration Services website is a good place for general information. It is updated regularly as laws and policies change regarding immigration. https://www.uscis.gov.

12. New York Times, "Government to Shut Down."

13. Stewart, *Immigration*, 57.

14. Stewart, *Immigration*, 57; Department of Homeland Security, DHS Organizational Chart.

United States Citizens and Naturalization

In one of the more generous provisions of immigration law, anyone born in the United States is automatically a citizen at birth.[15] Also, some people born outside the United States to United States Citizen parents are citizens at birth,[16] as are some individuals born in United States territories.[17] Birthright citizenship is derived from the Fourteenth Amendment to the Constitution and codified in the Immigration and Nationality Act.[18]

Immigrants become United States citizens through naturalization, the process of becoming a citizen. In general, someone who wants to naturalize must have resided in the United States for five years as a Lawful Permanent Resident prior to applying and should not have been absent from the United States for more than 6 months during those five years. The applicant has to pass a rigorous background examination and fill out a lengthy form detailing where they've lived and worked. They must demonstrate good moral character, as determined by a USCIS officer.[19] They are fingerprinted, and their naturalization application is compared to previous immigration applications to ensure each application is identical. The applicant must travel to a USCIS office to take a civics test and demonstrate competence in written and spoken English through writing answers to civics questions and engaging in conversation with a USCIS officer.[20] The immigrant must also demonstrate an attachment to the principles of the US Constitution.

---

15. Many immigrants have children who are citizens, while they themselves are Lawful Permanent Residents or are undocumented. Mixed-status families express significant anxiety on the stability of their family structure; these families are at risk of being separated by immigration detention or deportation. *See Haynes*, "Mixed-Status Families and the Threat of Deportation."

16. *See* Immigration and Nationality Act, 8 U.S.C. 1401.

17. *See* Immigration and Nationality Act, 8 U.S.C. 1401; Immigration and Nationality Act, 8 U.S.C. 1402; Immigration and Nationality Act, 8 U.S.C. 1403; Immigration and Nationality Act, 8 U.S.C. 1406; Immigration and Nationality Act, 8 U.S.C. 1407; Immigration and Nationality Act, 8 U.S.C. 1408; et al.

18. Immigration and Nationality Act, 8 U.S.C. 1401.

19. Immigration and Nationality Act, 8 U.S.C. 1427.

20. A notable exception to the English language requirement is the disability waiver, which waives the English requirement for immigrants who cannot and will not ever be able to learn English. This is based on federal regulations, which generally require the federal government to make accommodations for individuals who are disabled. *See* 6 Code of Federal Regulations 15.50. There are also exceptions for individuals who have lived in the United States for a significant period of time. *See* Immigration and Nationality Act, 8 U.S.C. 1423.

There are a number of bars to citizenship. Certain crimes, diseases, and even behaviors that have not been criminalized, such as adultery and drunkenness, can prevent an immigrant from naturalizing.[21] Some bars can be waived and others are permanent.

After passing each of these stages, the immigrant is invited to take the oath of citizenship at a naturalization ceremony. Citizenship confers a number of benefits; it gives the immigrant the right to vote and the right to hold a federal job and serve on jury duty. It opens up access to more public benefits for longer periods of time. Citizens may petition for family members to join them in the United States more easily, as will be described more fully below. Their children under 18 become citizens automatically. They can apply for and receive a United States passport, potentially giving them greater access to travel opportunities. Citizens cannot be deported, absent extreme circumstances.

Naturalization ceremonies are joyful occasions, representing many years of hard work, significant costs, and waiting for the immigrant. Each immigrant who naturalizes was first a Lawful Permanent Resident, which also represents many years of hard work, costs, and waiting, and will be detailed next.

Lawful Permanent Residents (LPR)

A Lawful Permanent Resident (LPR), or green card holder, is an immigrant who is permitted to remain in the United States for a specific or indefinite period of time. Some LPRs will be eligible to apply to naturalize after a certain number of years. There are two types of LPRs, those who obtain status abroad and then enter the United States through an overseas consulate and those who apply to become an LPR while remaining the United States. Immigrants can obtain a green card in multiple ways, though there are relatively few options in proportion to the number of individuals who want to immigrate.

Like applying for naturalization, applicants for green cards are subject to multiple levels of applications, fees, and interviews. Most applicants must have been inspected before entering the United States, which typically means they entered through a border (including a seaport or an international airport) and were admitted to the United States by an immigration officer. If an immigrant was not inspected before entering the United States, they must

21. Immigration and Nationality Act, 8 U.S.C. 1101(f).

leave the United States and be re-admitted through inspection at a consular office outside the United States before obtaining a green card.

There are a number of immigrants who are deemed inadmissible, who can never be granted permanent residency.[22] Inadmissibility can be based on the immigrant's health, criminal record, political affiliations, financial status or potential financial status, marriage status, or immigration status, among a few other reasons. These categories of inadmissibility apply to every visa listed here. As with bars to naturalization, some types of inadmissibility can be waived and other types are lifelong. Immigrants who have entered the country unlawfully might be permanently barred from obtaining a green card. Immigrants with any type of criminal conviction, regardless of how small or how long ago it occurred, any use of illegal drugs, or even mental health diseases can prevent an immigrant from obtaining a green card.

The most common ways to obtain a green card are through family petitions, employment visas, entering as a refugee, obtaining a diversity visa, being granted asylum, and being a victim of crime. Typically, an immigrant enters the United States on a specific visa and then can adjust status to become an LPR while in the United States.

Family Petitions

Family petitions are by far the most common way to immigrate to the United States. As a result of the Immigration and Nationality Act of 1965, the United States immigration system is centered on reuniting families.[23] In 2017, over 65% of applicants for green cards came through family sponsorship.[24] There are two categories of family petitions.

Those in the first category can obtain a green card as soon as their application is approved. There is no wait other than the standard wait for application processing times. This first category includes spouses of U.S. Citizens, children of U.S. citizens, parents of U.S. citizens who are at least 21 years old, and widows or widowers of citizens.[25]

Those in the second category face the longest road; they must apply for and then wait on an available visa. This category includes: unmarried

---

22. Immigration and Nationality Act, 8 U.S.C. 1182.
23. *See* Tienda, "Multiplying Diversity," 727.
24. United States, *Yearbook*, Table 6.
25. See Immigration and Nationality Act, 8 U.S.C. 1151(b)(2)(A)(i).

sons and daughters of U.S. citizens; spouses, children, and unmarried sons and daughters (21 years and older) of permanent residents; married sons and daughters of U.S. citizens; and brothers and sisters of adult U.S. citizens.[26] Each month, the Department of State publishes the waiting list for those who apply to enter the country as a relative of a U.S. citizen in one of these categories.[27] Each category of applicant has a set number of immigrants who can come to the United States each month. Further, there are separate, longer, lines for those from Mexico, China, the Philippines, and India. When a category becomes full, a waiting list forms.

Some of the waiting lists are astronomically long. As an example, as of January 2019, the line for Filipino married sons and daughters of United States Citizens to immigrate to the United States is backed up to July 22, 1995. Unfortunately, that's not the whole picture, as the visa bulletin doesn't move every month and sometimes moves backwards depending on how many people file for a visa in each category.[28]

As an additional barrier, for low income immigrants, sponsors must meet certain income guidelines, proving they can support their joining family member. The family sponsor becomes financially responsible for their immigrating family member and creditors can establish claims against these family sponsors. The sponsors must also pay the application fees and attorney fees for each person immigrating, which can total thousands of dollars.

Immigrating as a family member is the easiest and most common way to enter the United States, but often, even when a family member could qualify to immigrate, the sponsor in the United States simply does not have the resources to reunite their family

26. United States, "Visa Bulletin For January 2019."

27. This waiting list is called a Visa Bulletin. United States, "Visa Bulletin for January 2019."

28. For an explanation on visa retrogression, *see* United States Citizenship and Immigration Services, "Visa Retrogression," https://www.uscis.gov/green-card/green-card-processes-and-procedures/visa-availability-priority-dates/visa-retrogression.

Employment Visas

Employment visas can be short-term or extended into permanency.[29] Both the employer and employee must fit into certain categories and there are a number of employment visas for both unskilled and skilled labor.[30]

There are five broad categories of employment-based immigration: priority workers; members of professions holding advanced degrees or persons of exceptional availability; skills workers, professionals, and other workers; certain special immigrations; and those creating employment.[31] These categories are capped by country to encourage more diversity in the incoming work force, though there are exceptions and per-country caps can be exceeded in some cases.[32]

Many immigrants with an employment-based visa can apply for a green card after a certain period of time and include their family members on their petition.[33] However, like the family preference categories, there is often a significant wait.[34] The same four countries, Mexico, China, India, and the Philippines all face longer wait times than the general immigrant population. The same bars of inadmissibility apply as well.

Refugees

Refugees are individuals who do not live in their country of nationality and who are unable or unwilling to return to their home country because of persecution or a well-founded fear of persecution on account of race, religion, nationality, membership in a particular social group, or political opinion.[35] They must be of special humanitarian value to the United States, they must be admissible to the United States generally, and must not be firmly resettled in a third country.

29. *See generally* United States Citizenship and Immigration Services, "Working in the US."

30. Stewart, *Immigration*, 63.

31. *See generally* United States Citizenship and Immigration Services, "Working in the US."

32. Immigration and Nationality Act, 8 U.S.C. 1151.

33. *See generally* United States Citizenship and Immigration Services, "Green Card for Employment-Based Immigrants."

34. United States, "Visa Bulletin for January 2019."

35. Immigration and Nationality Act, 8 U.S.C. 1151.

Immigrating to the United States as a refugee is a lengthy process, with multiple security screenings and re-checks of biometric information.[36] Refugees are first identified while abroad by the United Nations High Commission for Refugees (UNHCR), often while living in a refugee camp. Refugees don't apply or even state a preference to be resettled but are independently chosen by UNHCR. And, if chosen for resettlement, refugees cannot choose or state a preference as to where they are ultimately resettled.

After being identified and chosen for resettlement, the refugee is then referred to a Refugee Support Center, who begins biometric screenings and interviews. Next, the refugee is interviewed in person by a USCIS officer and USCIS reviews and initiates additional biometric screenings as needed and reviews the refugee application form. The Refugee Support Center then prepares the refugee for travel, conducts medical exams, and connects the refugee with a resettlement agency in the United States. The refugee is screened again before boarding an international flight to the United States. Finally, the refugee is screened once more by Customs and Border Patrol before entering the United States.

If a refugee travels to the United States without their family, they can petition for their family members to join them once they reach the United States. Refugees can work as soon as they enter the United States but must wait one year before applying for a green card.

Only a small percentage of refugees worldwide are resettled into third countries and the United States has traditionally led the world in formal resettlement of refugees. In 2017, there were 68.5 million forcibly displaced people worldwide, 25.4 million of whom were identified as refugees by UNHCR. But, only 102,800 refugees were resettled worldwide.[37] This is why when the President cuts refugee admissions, it is very significant.

Refugee entries are capped by the Executive Branch, approved specifically by the President by way of Presidential Declaration after consultation with Congress.[38] President Trump set a 45,000 cap in 2018 and has proposed a 30,000 cap for 2019.[39] In contrast, under President Obama

---

36. *See* United States Citizenship and Immigration Services, "Refugee Processing and Security Screening."

37. United Nations High Commissioner for Refugees, "Global Trends: Forced Displacement in 2017."

38. *See* United States President. Presidential Determination.

39. United States Department of State, *Proposed Refugee Admission for Fiscal Year 2019.*

in 2016, 84,994 refugees were admitted into the United States, still a low number comparatively.[40]

Diversity Visa

The diversity visa program was initiated to encourage individuals from countries with low rates of immigration to immigrate to the United States.[41] Currently, most of these immigrants come from African nations. After applying, potential immigrants are chosen by random in a lottery to immigrate to the United States. The same processing and security check requirements apply for individuals who obtain diversity visas. Diversity visas are numerically capped at roughly 50,000 per year. In 2018, over 19 million people applied for the diversity lottery and 49,976 ultimately immigrated.[42]

Asylum

Asylees are refugees who are identified and admitted while in the United States rather than while living abroad. Like refugees, asylees must have been persecuted, or have a well-founded fear of future persecution, based on their race, religion, nationality, membership in a particular social group, or political opinion. The main difference is that asylees must arrive in the United States on their own and apply for asylum within a year of arrival rather than being identified abroad by UNHCR.

The first and biggest barrier to applying for asylum is actually getting to the United States. Most developing countries require significant documentation before granting visas to travel to the United States, including requiring proof that the applicant has the financial capacity to return to their home country and proof that the applicant has significant ties to their home country that would encourage them to return, such as owning a business or owning a significant amount of property. Hopeful asylees can also cross an international border by foot or car and present themselves to Custom and Border Patrol as asylee applicants.

Applicants for asylum may add their spouse or unmarried children under 21 to their application or may apply for them to immigrate after they've

---

40. United States Department of State, *Proposed Refugee Admission for Fiscal Year 2019*.

41. Immigration and Nationality Act, 8 U.S.C. 1153(c).

42. United States, "Diversity Visa Program, DV 2016–2018."

been granted asylum. Applicants can also obtain work authorization while they wait for their application for asylum to be adjudicated. Applicants for asylum go through a rigorous background check. They are fingerprinted and are interviewed by a USCIS officer to verify their application.

One of the most significant challenges to obtaining asylum is meeting the fear of persecution or actual persecution requirement.[43] The persecution has to be personal and based on an individual characteristic.[44] As an illustration, an asylee applicant from Uganda cannot cite a high murder and violence rate as their well-founded fear in support of their application for asylum. However, an asylee applicant who is homosexual, who can document that they are homosexual, and can also document that homosexual individuals are targeted and persecuted by the Ugandan government, would have a case for asylum. The dangerous conditions in an individual's home country are not relevant unless the person has a specific reason to fear for their own safety based on their race, religion, nationality, membership in a particular social group, or political opinion.

Visas for Victims of Crimes

U Visas are visas set aside for certain victims of crime. "Congress recognized that victims who do not have legal status may be reluctant to help in the investigation or prosecution of criminal activity for fear of removal from the United States."[45] Congress created U Visas to encourage undocumented immigrants to report crimes in immigrant communities. U Visas are intended to be mutually beneficial for law enforcement and the undocumented immigrants. The victim has to have suffered substantial physical or mental abuse and must be of past, current, or future benefit to law enforcement in the prosecution of that crime.[46]

Victims submit an application with general demographic information and also a signed form from law enforcement, certifying that they helped in

43. See Hong, "Weaponizing Misery," 568.

44. See United States Citizenship and Immigration Services, "Asylum," https://www.uscis.gov/humanitarian/refugees-asylum/asylum. "Asylum Law", 132 Harvard Law Review, 803 (2018).

45. United States Department of Homeland Security, *U Visa Law Enforcement Certification Resource Guide*, 2.

46. See United States Department of Homeland Security, *U Visa Law Enforcement Certification Resource Guide*, 1.

the prosecution of that crime.[47] A signed certification is necessary to obtain U status, though not sufficient. The applicant is still required to comply with the additional application steps and background checks.

U Visa applicants are permitted to apply for their immediate family members to receive green cards as well. Currently, there is a 10,000 cap on the number of U Visas that are granted annually; there was a five-year waiting list at the end of 2018 and a two-year backlog to even get on the waiting list.[48]

In addition to U Visas, victims of crime can also apply for T Visas, which are visas for victims of human trafficking; VAWA, a petition for spouses who have been the victim of domestic violence; and a few other related temporary statuses. Though these visas come with significant benefits, the opportunity to obtain a green card and ultimately become a citizen, it requires first that an immigrant has encountered tremendous suffering.

Other Assorted Visas

There are a number of other visas that provide green cards, but the types listed above are by far the most common. The remaining types include, but are not limited to, certain Iraqis and Afghanis who have assisted in the wars there; parolees; children born abroad to certain parents; cancellation of removal; and a few other varied types of visas. The same bars of admissibility apply to each of these.

LPRs are able to access some public benefits for a prescribed amount of time and are usually permitted to remain in the United States indefinitely absent extreme circumstances. LPRs are also at risk of forfeiting their status if they leave the United States for a significant period of time. Becoming an LPR is a necessary first step to eventually applying to naturalize. If the immigrant does not fit into one of these categories, they may not lawfully immigrate.

---

47. *See* United States Department of Homeland Security, *U Visa Law Enforcement Certification Resource Guide*, 2–8. The unfortunate reality of the U Visa is that not every law enforcement officer will sign these necessary forms.

48. You can check current wait times at: United States, *The Visa Bulletin*, https://travel.state.gov/content/travel/en/legal/visa-lawo/visa-bulletin.html.

The Undocumented

The undocumented population is significant but does not make up the majority of immigrants in the United States. Only about 24% of immigrants are undocumented.[49] In 2016, there were an estimated eleven million undocumented immigrants in the United States, with approximately half from Mexico.[50] Over seven million of the almost eleven million are in the workforce, creating a huge shadow economy.[51] Significantly, it's estimated that as many as 66% of the undocumented population have lived in the United States for ten years or longer.[52] For the past ten years, most of the new undocumented population overstayed a temporary visa rather than crossed a border unlawfully and the undocumented population has declined significantly in general.[53]

For many of these undocumented immigrants, they will never have an opportunity to gain lawful status unless something significant changes in the immigration system. Many of these undocumented immigrants have children and parents in the United States and communities that depend on them. They are an integral part of our community and our workforce. Meaningful reform is necessary to bring this population out of the shadows.

Deferred Action for Childhood Arrivals

On June 15, 2012, President Barack Obama announced Deferred Action for Childhood Arrivals (DACA), which granted prosecutorial discretion to some undocumented immigrants who were brought to the United States unlawfully when they were children. Prosecutorial discretion means that these undocumented immigrants who are granted DACA will not be deported.

DACA is not an immigration status, but only discretionary protection from deportation and the authority to work. DACA is entirely discretional, can be rescinded at any time, and it cannot be converted into a green card or citizenship. Individuals with DACA are simply in a

49. López, "Key Findings About U.S. Immigrants."

50. Krogstad, "5 Facts About Illegal Immigration in the U.S." DHS estimates 12 million in 2015. *See* Baker, *Estimates of the Illegal Alien Population Residing in the United States: January 2015.*

51. Krogstad, "5 Facts About Illegal Immigration in the U.S."

52. Krogstad, "5 Facts About Illegal Immigration in the U.S."

53. Warren, "US Undocumented Population."

temporary state of lack of immigration status that is acknowledged by the United States Government.

Currently, for an individual to obtain DACA, they must have been under the age of 31 on June 15, 2012; have arrived in the United States before they turned 16; have continuously resided in the United States from June 15, 2007, until the time of application; were physically present in the United States on June 15, 2012; have had no lawful status on June 15, 2012; have a high school education or equivalent or have been honorably discharged from the United States Coast Guard or Armed Forces; and have not been convicted of a felony, significant misdemeanor, or three or more misdemeanors.

As of February 2018, 800,000 individuals have benefited from DACA protection.[54] Though the vast majority are Mexican nationals or from Latin American countries, the rest of the DACA population consists of more than twenty-four nationalities.[55] 800,000 young people who were brought here as children now have the opportunity to work and attend college knowing they're employable after graduation. Though DACA has helped many people, it's not enough. Young people who were slightly too old or who entered the United States with their parents since DACA was announced are left out of this safeguard.

Obama instituted DACA when Congress could not pass the DREAM act;[56] the major difference between DACA and the DREAM act is that the DREAM act would have provided a pathway to citizenship for this population, whereas DACA provides no pathway to permanent immigration status. DACA was intended to be a stopgap measure until Congress could pass the DREAM act. Though providing a pathway for citizenship for those brought across the border at a young age has received broad bipartisan support,[57] Congress has been unable to pass any reform in this area.

54. "Key Facts on Individuals Eligible for the Deferred Action for Childhood Arrivals (DACA) Program," Kaiser Family Foundation; López, "Key Facts about Unauthorized Immigrants Enrolled in DACA."

55. United States Citizenship and Immigration Services, "Number of Form I-821D, Consideration of Deferred Action for Childhood Arrivals, by Fiscal Year, Quarter, Intake and Case Status Fiscal Year 2012-2018 (September 30, 2018)."

56. Obama, "Remarks by the President on Immigration."

57. *See* Obama, "Remarks by the President on Immigration."

Why Does It Matter?

These are functionally all the options for immigrating to the United States. That nearly every immigration option can be summarized in a single chapter is meant to emphasize that there are not many options. Further, many of the "options" that exist are not realistic, as they require significant wait times; or they require that an immigrant has suffered substantial abuse while in the United States; or they require an immigrant to have been persecuted by their government while in their home country. Though there are few options to lawfully immigrate, there are even fewer *desirable* options to legally immigrate to the United States.

Immigration law is contentious. Both sides of the aisle cannot even agree on what to call those who enter the country unlawfully, let alone any type of reform to improve the immigration system. Further, though there might be two broad camps of thought, there is a wide disparity of views even within those two camps.[58] Within both sides, people disagree as to whom should be allowed to adjust status or naturalize while in the United States unlawfully; there is disagreement on caps on immigration from certain countries; there are those who oppose deporting criminals and those who favor deporting parents. There are those who oppose refugee admission and those who think we are doing far too little to mitigate the global crisis of displaced peoples.

But also, immigration law is personal. When I think of restricting asylum, I think of my client who was raped by a soldier while her mother and father were killed in the same room. When I think about undocumented immigrants, I think of my client who, as a twelve-year-old, was trafficked across the southern border by a coyote and made her way to family in Ohio. She got pregnant along the way. When I think of family petitions, I remember explaining the visa bulletin to a pair of brothers. I watched them as they came to the realization that the enormous waiting list meant that they would never see their other brother again.

We cannot forget the people behind the immigration structures we have created. We cannot forget the humanity behind the numbers. Understanding what the current system is will help us advocate for a fairer, more rational, set of laws, a set of laws that acknowledges the humanity in each immigrant.

58. *See* Powell, *Immigration*, 51.

6

Immigration and the Biblical Migrant Narratives

—J. Dwayne Howell

R ecent statistics by the United Nations High Commission for Refugees
state that there are 68.5 million forcibly displaced people in the world
today, forced out of their homeland due to military, political, and economic
factors.[1] This is the largest number of refugees ever recorded. A leading
cause for this number is the refugee crisis that has emerged out of the ongoing civil war in Syria. Add to this number of displaced people the 232
million immigrants in the world today, those who have voluntarily left
their countries of origin to pursue life elsewhere.[2] As many nations seek to
respond to the rising number of migrants, opposition to aiding them has
also emerged. The larger numbers of refugees and immigrants have led to a
rise in calls to reform immigration systems. In light of the tragic events of
September 11, 2001, many citizens of the United States have re-evaluated

1 United Nations Office of the High Commissioner of Human Rights (UNCHR)
https://www.unhcr.org/figures-at-a-glance.html These are people who have been
forced out of their homeland for the various reasons. Warfare is a dominant reason.
Fifty-four percent of the refugees are from three countries: Syria, Afghanistan and
Somalia. Also, the 2015 report shows a 5.8 million person increase of 2014. Cf. "With
1 human in every 113 affected, forced displacement hits record high," http://www.
unhcr.org/en-us/news/press/2016/6/5763ace54/1-human-113-affected-forced-displa-
cement-hits-record-high.html

2. UNCHR, "Migration and Human Rights: People on the Move."

their relations with those from other countries. The increase in xenophobia and anger toward immigrants entering the country have led to hateful and violent responses from some American citizens resulting in the suffering of many. New policies have caused mass detention and family separation.[3] The tragedy is compounded by the rise in hate crimes against migrants including American citizens of foreign birth or ancestry.[4]

In the present national (and international) situation, what is an appropriate faith-based response to the immigrant? One consideration is that many of the biblical narratives are stories of migration, people constantly on the move, looking for a safe homeland. These traditions are found in both Jewish and Christian literature and serve as a reminder of past deliverance for their adherents. Realizing the number of migrant stories in the Bible as they pertain to the effects of displacement, what are the implications for the treatment of the immigrant entering our countries today? Two stories about migration, the Abraham narrative and the exodus narrative, serve as foundational stories for the establishment of Israel in the Old Testament.[5]

The Problem

Recent political activity in the United States has led to a rise in the distrust of the immigrant. Calls are made by some to build walls and to close the borders to those in certain religious or ethnic groups. Statements have also been made about deporting the estimated eleven million undocumented immigrants. A fear of those especially from Middle Eastern descent, in part a carryover from the 9/11 attacks, has been accentuated by recent violence and mass shootings in the United States and abroad. Elsewhere, anti-immigration sentiment was part of the impetus behind the recent Brexit vote in Great Britain.[6] Other European countries are feeling similar outrage from immigration opponents. There is a growing belief among these groups that

3. Over one-half of the migrants are children. Note also the combined number of refugees and immigrants would be 4% of the world's population, or 1 out of every 25 people.

4. Winston, "Report Says List of 'Islamophobic Groups' Reaches New High".

5. Abraham and the exodus are used as an example for biblical migrant narratives. Other narratives include but are not limited to Ruth, the Exile, the Diaspora, Jesus (birth narrative and itinerant ministry), and Paul.

6. Guyjoco, "Cardinal Vincent Nichols Condemns 'Upsurge' of Racism and Hatred in Brexit Aftermath."

immigrants are a drain on a nation's economy and that possible terrorists may be embedded with the migrants.

American history attests to similar fears against those who migrated to the United States over time, including but not limited to Irish/Catholics, Italians, Eastern Europeans, Chinese, and Jews. Laws based on quotas restricting the migration and naturalization of people in the United States were in place until the 1960s.[7] It is ironic that the United States motto *E Pluribus Unum* "out of many one" acknowledges the multiple nationalities present in the United States.[8] In the 1950s, in part due to an enmity with Communism and its perceived atheist views, the motto was changed to "In God We Trust." These two mottos do not need to be mutually exclusive. However, there is a danger of invoking the divine by attempting to nationalize God and believing whatever a nation does is sanctioned by God.

What is to be a faith-based response to immigration? Since 2003 I have been studying immigration as it pertains to the Old Testament, especially Lev 19:34 and 35:

> [33] When an alien resides with you in your land, you shall not oppress the alien. [34] The alien who resides with you shall be to you as the citizen among you; you shall love the alien as yourself, for you were aliens in the land of Egypt: I am the LORD your God.

A paper on the treatment of the immigrant in Leviticus 19 is required reading in my one of my masters' classes. I have been taken aback by some who respond that "we are no longer under the law" and that this passage no longer applies to one's understanding of immigration issues today. I have also had the passage's efficacy questioned by church members. This in consideration that Lev 19:33 is in direct parallel with 19:18: "but you shall love your neighbor as yourself," which Jesus said was the second great commandment (Mt. 22:34–40). Friends afraid of terrorists and believing that immigrants are a drain on society, believe that Christianity requires a different response to immigration today. I have found that many anti-immigration views expressed by friends, students, commentators and politicians are often based on ill-informed opinion.[9]

---

7. Ewing, "Opportunity and Exclusion: A Brief History of U.S. Immigration Policy."

8. By an act from Congress in 1795, this motto appears on the Seal of the United States and currency.

9. See appendix for a list of readings concerning immigration myths and facts.

Migrant Nature of Biblical Narratives

One way to approach a faith-based understanding of immigration is to real-ize the migrant nature of many of the biblical narratives in both the Hebrew canon and Christian canon. The New Testament writers emphasize the concept of the Kingdom of God and the temporal nature of this earth. The Hebrew Bible contains many narratives about the people of God moving to-ward a promised land. The migration described in the Hebrew Bible follows similar migration patterns of other ethnic groups in the ancient Near East. There are various reasons for the migration patterns during this time.[10] First is the natural movement of people in and out of the region.[11] Today, as well as then, groups of semi-nomadic and nomadic people travel throughout the region. A second reason for migration arose out of natural causes such as drought, famine and disease. These frequently occurred in the ancient Near East leading to mass migration of people groups looking for food and relief.[12] A third reason for the migration of people would be the constant warfare in the lands of the ancient Near East.[13] Refugees would commonly search for peaceful areas to settle. Today, many flee their countries due to violence of war and its threats to personal security. Finally, people would migrate to escape from personal crimes and the vengeance of others.[14]

Walter Brueggemann sees two movements in the history of Israel. First, Israel presumes upon the gift of land and is ultimately expelled from the land. Secondly, Israel lives in anticipation of a gift of land it does not yet possess. Thus, Israel's history is in a constant tension between "expul-sion and anticipation."[15] This is exemplified in Genesis as chapters 1–11 displays both the gaining and the losing of the land and in chapters 12–50 Abraham and his descendants anticipate the divine gift of land. The

---

10. See *KB* 1:201. See also Kellerman, 443.

11. Abraham refers to himself as a *gēr* (Gen. 15:13; 23:4).

12. Joseph (Gen. 43–50), Ruth (Elimelech takes his wife and sons to Moab from Bethlehem during a time of famine. Also, Ruth is a widow and an immigrant in Israel when she returns with her mother-in-law Naomi. She even partakes in the practice of collecting "gleanings" as prescribed for the poor and immigrant in Lev. 19:10.

13. In Judges 9, the Gibeonites trick the Israelites into providing protection by pre-tending to flee an advancing army.

14. Exod. 2:11–22. See also Exod. 18:3. Here Moses explains the name of his son Gershom (*gēršôm*) "because I have been a sojourner (immigrant) in a foreign land" (*kî . . . gēr hāyîtî bĕĕrĕs nākĕrîyāh*).

15. Brueggemann, *Land*, 15.

anticipation continues in the exodus narratives as Israel leaves Egypt and moves toward the Promised Land.

The Abraham and exodus narratives are both migration stories and are foundational for understanding the beginning of Israel. Israel's confession of faith, Deut 26:5–9, centers on these two narratives:

> 5 you shall make this response before the LORD your God: "A wandering Aramean was my ancestor; he went down into Egypt and lived there as an alien, few in number, and there he became a great nation, mighty and populous. 6 When the Egyptians treated us harshly and afflicted us, by imposing hard labor on us, 7 we cried to the LORD, the God of our ancestors; the LORD heard our voice and saw our affliction, our toil, and our oppression. 8 The LORD brought us out of Egypt with a mighty hand and an outstretched arm, with a terrifying display of power, and with signs and wonders; 9 and he brought us into this place and gave us this land, a land flowing with milk and honey.

The Wandering Aramean—Abraham

The Abraham stories (Gen 12–24) begin the Patriarch narratives of Genesis (Gen 12–50) which recount the movement of the patriarchs out of Mesopotamia through Palestine and concludes with Abraham's descendants living in Egypt. From the beginning, the Abraham narratives describe the migration of his family. Abraham is actually first introduced in the genealogy of Terah, his father, in Gen 11:27–32, who moves his family from Ur in southeast Mesopotamia to Haran in northwest Mesopotamia. Normally the patriarchal families were extended families living together. It is in this context that the Abraham stories begin. Genesis 12:1–3 is God's call and covenant with Abraham:

> 1 Now the LORD said to Abram, "Go from your country and your kindred and your father's house to the land that I will show you. 2 I will make of you a great nation, and I will bless you, and make your name great, so that you will be a blessing. 3 I will bless those who bless you, and the one who curses you I will curse; and in you all the families of the earth shall be blessed."

The Abrahamic covenant seeks to unify the people once again after the Tower of Babel story (Gen 11:1–9) through a promise: "and in you all the families of the earth shall be blessed." (v. 3). The covenant, based on obedience, begins with the promise of land (v. 1), followed by a promise of descendants which is important since he and his wife Sarah have no children (11:30). The possession of land and having descendants to pass the land down to are two important elements in the ancient Near Eastern culture.

The Abraham narratives are placed in the early second millennium BCE, a time of a mass migration out of Mesopotamia toward the south along the Mediterranean Sea.[16] Thus, Abraham is following the natural migration of people in that day. As a migrant, he faced similar problems as others and relied on the hospitality of those he met. He dealt with threats to his family (Gen 12:10–20; 20:1–18) and dissension among his family (Gen 13:1–18). The entire Abraham narrative is about seeking a land in which to settle but never accomplishing that quest. In requesting a burial site for Sarah, Abraham states " I am a stranger (i.e. "immigrant") and an alien residing among you; give me property among you for a burying place, so that I may bury my dead out of my sight" (Gen 23:4). Upon his death, the only land that Abraham possessed was Sarah's burial plot. Abraham never fully realizes the promise given in Gen 12:1–3, underlining a parallel of the uncertainty between ancient Near Eastern migration and a similar uncertainty of migration today, since many do not reach their full destination.

The Exodus Narrative

The Israelite sojourn in Egypt, their eventual release from captivity, and their migration through the wilderness is the second part of the creed found in Deut 26:5–9. The exodus narrative spans from Exodus through Deuteronomy in the Pentateuch. While the Israelites are not in possession of the Promised Land at the end of the Pentateuch, Deuteronomy anticipates the entry into the land and Joshua shares its fulfillment. The exodus from Egypt, the wilderness wandering, the preparation to enter the land, and the eventual conquest of the land (Joshua) become the central redemptive act of the Old Testament. It is the event that later writers refer to when Israel loses it hope or when it becomes faithless.

The time spent in Egypt has a two-fold significance for Israel. First, their ancestors had traveled to Egypt during a time of famine while Joseph, one of the patriarchs, was a leader in Egypt (Gen 46:1—47:28). However, once they had settled in Egypt and after the time of famine a Pharaoh came

16. Bright, *A History of Israel*, 80ff.

to power who "did not know Joseph" (Exod 1:8) and oppressed the Israelites in Egypt out of fear that they may do harm to the Egyptians:

> He said to his people, "Look, the Israelite people are more numer-
> ous and more powerful than we. Come, let us deal shrewdly with
> them, or they will increase and, in the event of war, join our en-
> emies and fight against us and escape from the land." Therefore,
> they set taskmasters over them to oppress them with forced labor.
> They built supply cities, Pithom and Rameses, for Pharaoh. (Exod
> 1:9–11; cf. 1:9—2:25)

Thus, Israel's ancestors in Egypt experienced both the hospitality of
Egypt in time of need and the tyranny of Egypt during a time of servitude.
The story demonstrates how a non-indigenous group can be enslaved by
the native inhabitants in the land. The story also includes reports of geno-
cide to control the enslaved population (Exod 1:15–22). The exodus of the
Hebrews out of Egypt is similar to many today who are trying to escape
persecution in their own land.

The travelers encountered many problems in their journey.[17] First,
they face a lack of provisions as they traveled. Without a divine intervention they would have starved in the wilderness (Exod 16; cf. Num 11).
Migrants today often suffer from the lack of provisions and rely on the
hospitality of those in whose land they travel. Some laws prohibit giving
such aid to migrants.[18]

A second problem the Hebrews faced was internal dissension. The
"caravan" of Hebrews leaving Egypt for the Promised Land was not a ho-
mogenous group of dedicated travelers. The time in the wilderness, portrayed as a 40-year journey, shows Israel disoriented and distrustful as the
people migrate toward the Promised Land. They are disoriented as they
are brought out of a land that had provided for them but only at the cost
of oppression. They are distrustful as they are led through the wilderness

---

17. Brueggemann, 29–37. Brueggemann discusses the tension between the wilderness dissent and the Promised Land anticipation found in the exodus narrative using a
comparison of Exodus 16 and Numbers 14.)

18. Rafael Carranza, "Four aid volunteers found guilty of dropping off water, food for
migrants in Arizona desert." Four from the humanitarian group, No More Deaths, were
convicted of trespassing on federal lands when they left jugs of water and cans of beans
throughout the Cabeza Prieta National Wildlife Refuge in southeastern Arizona, an area
known for many human remains being found annually. The government claimed that
they had not procured proper permits to enter into the area. It also emphasized that it
had four help station through the refuge to aid people.

to a land, they do not know but that offers them freedom. The distrust led to dissension among the migrants and toward their leaders. At times the Israelites preferred to return to Egypt, to the familiar, which offered some comfort despite the oppression. At other times the Israelites revolted and sought a change of leadership, most notably when Aaron and Miriam sought to wrest control from their brother Moses (Num. 12). Many of the migrants today are not organized groups of people. Many are simply brought together just by their longing for a better life.

A third problem faced on the wilderness journey was attacks that sought to halt their progress. They were first pursued by the Egyptians but escaped at the crossing of the Sea of Reeds (Exod 13:17—15:21). Before entering the Sinai wilderness, they were attacked by the Amalekites (Exod 17:8–16). Other military battles included attacks by Sihon and Og, who refused the Israelites passage through their lands (Num 21:21–35) and Balak, king of Moab, who attempted to have a curse placed on the Israelites by Balaam, a Mesopotamian Holy man (Num 22:1—24:25). A natural fear occurs when one's homeland is being entered by other groups; a fear of what changes can occur. However, xenophobic reactions to the stranger as being terrorists and drug dealers can cause nations to refuse aid, cut off entry, and threaten military retaliation against migrant caravans. Migrants are, likewise, attacked by gangs and others seeking to take advantage of their vulnerability as they travel through the land.

Both the Abraham narratives and the exodus narratives display a hope for a better life by the migration to a new land. Both narratives show the obstacles that were faced in these travels, both external and internal. Similar problems are faced by migrants today as they seek for a better life.

"Living in Memory"

The Abraham and exodus migration stories in the Pentateuch remind the Israelites that they were once immigrants in the lands where they dwelt. A common theme in the exodus narrative is that Israel is to remember that they were immigrants in the land of Egypt and how God provided for them. "In the wilderness Yahweh provides when there seems to be no available provision (see Gen 22:14), life is rooted in impossibility."[19] It is out of this memory that they are called upon to help those who are immigrants and refugees in their land. In *A People Called: The Growth of Community in*

19. Brueggemann, 41.

the Bible, Paul D. Hanson sees the early community of Israel as "living in memory" of the exodus.[20] Central to that memory would be God's compassion in the act of deliverance. Hanson believes that this memory should lead Israel to practice "compassionate justice." Thus, the Egypt sojourn reminded the Israelites of the importance of hospitality for the ones who would now sojourn in their land.[21]

For you were immigrants in the land of Egypt. Israel is reminded that they were once in a similar situation as the immigrant in their land. The theme is found in Exodus (20:21; 23:9), Leviticus (19:34; 25:23) and Deuteronomy (10:19).[22] In these passages Israel is likewise reminded that it had sojourned in Egypt. Exod 23:9 states that the Israelites know the "heart" of the immigrant because of their time in Egypt. Leviticus 19:34 calls for the Israelites to treat the immigrant as a citizen in the land. Leviticus 25:23 reminds Israel that the land belongs to God making Israel a continual immigrant even in its own land.[23] Jacob Milgrom observes "Put it another way, the laws work to define Israel's present identity in terms of its past status and its future goals."[24]

Hospitality is the basis of Israel's responsibility to care for the immigrant and is an important part of everyday life in the ancient Near East. Unlike our concept of hospitality today (clean sheets and one's bed turned down with a complimentary chocolate on the pillow), hospitality in the ancient Near East is a matter of life and death.[25] Hostile conditions and

20. Hanson, *A People Called*, 45. In this section Hanson is actually dealing with Exod. 22:20b and its relation to the Covenant Code.

21. In several biblical passages the Israelites are reminded that they are still strangers/sojourners in the land because the land belongs to God (Lev. 25:23; 1 Chr 29:15; Pss 39:12 [v. 13 in Hebrew] and 119:19).

22. Each of the passages in Exodus, Leviticus, and Deuteronomy are found in the three major codes of the Pentateuch: The Covenant Code (Exod 20:22—23:19—one of the oldest Israelites legal codes); The Deuteronomic Code (Deut. 4:44–26:8, 28:1–68); and the Priestly Code (Exod 25:1—Num 10:10). See also Martin-Achard, "*gvr*," 309. Martin-Achard dates the references as follows: Exod 22:20b is the oldest followed by Deut 10:19 and finally Lev 19:34. He views Lev 19:34b as developing from Deut 10:19.

23. Milgrom, "The Alien in Your Midst," 18.

24. Milgrom, *Leviticus*, 1605.

25. See Malina, "Hospitality," 96–99. Malina's article deals primarily with the New Testament concept of hospitality but is also applicable to its practice in the ancient Near East.

The practice of hospitality in the ancient New East is still being carried out in the Middle East today. The lifestyle of the Bedouin peoples provides insights to the practice of hospitality in the Middle East today. See Lila Lughood, *Veiled Sentiments*. The author, a woman, describes her travels in Bedouin groups and their various practices, including

hostile relations between peoples groups place those traveling through the land at the mercy of the native people of a given territory. The temptation to take advantage of the less fortunate, including the immigrant, is likewise seen in the warning against using false measures in Lev 19:35–36.

Milgrom observes that the call to also care for the immigrant who is *settling in the land* appears to be unique to the literature of the Bible.[26] As with the poor, disabled, widows, and orphans, the immigrant can easily be taken advantage of in the land. The immigrant enters the land both homeless and landless.[27] In order to survive, the immigrant often becomes indebted to another and ends up a slave to that person.

The Pentateuch sets forward the treatment of the immigrant by the Israelites. John R. Spenser notes, however, that while equal treatment was to be the norm, "the sojourner did not enjoy the same social status as that of the Israelites."[28] Spenser notes that the immigrant:

1. has been singled out for biblical legislation;

2. differs in Israelite society;

3. is listed last in the fourth commandment in Exod 20:10, perhaps reflecting social status;

4. is often mentioned in association with the widow, orphan and poor (Lev 23:22; Deut 10:18; 24:17, 19; Jer 7:6; 22:3; Ezek 22:7, 9; Zech 7:10; Pss 94:6; 146:9).[29]

Hesitancy to aid the immigrant in the land may arise from the possible repercussions of such an act. Utmost among those concerns is that the

---

hospitality. See also Bailey, *Bedouin Poetry from Sinai to the Negev*. This book contains several Bedouin poems that deal specifically with hospitality.

26. Milgrom, *Leviticus,* 1627. See also Gowan, 343. Instructions to care for the poor citizens in one's community can be found in the Code of Hammurabi, ca. 1700 BCE (see Peterson, "The Widow, the Orphan, and the Poor in the Old Testament and Extrabiblical Literature," 226). Such instructions can be found in the Egyptian Instructions of Amen-em-ope, ca. 1250–1000 B.C.E. (See Oden, ed. *And You Welcomed Me,* 17.)

27. Milgrom, *Leviticus,* 1626, "It should never be forgotten that concern for the underprivileged, the poor, the widow, the orphan and the alien is consistently reiterated throughout the scripture." See Pohl, *Making Room,* 28. Pohl notes that immigrants were "landless in an agrarian society where land was usually distributed by inheritance and where access to land was essential to life."

28. Spenser, 104.

29. Ibid.

immigrants that are aided may in return become one's enemy.[30] However, little, if anything, is said in the Old Testament concerning the danger that the immigrant presents. Leviticus 25:42–53 deals with the redemption of an Israelite who has sold himself into slavery to a prosperous immigrant. However, this was not the norm.[31] The immigrant is most often grouped with the less fortunate of society, especially widows and orphans. The primary concern of the text is the care for the less fortunate in society. Due to the dangers faced by strangers, communities were encouraged to care for the immigrants in their land. The scripture is more concerned about the proper treatment of the immigrant than about the possible risks that may emerge from offering aid to the immigrant.

Conclusion

The biblical migrant narratives are a common theme through the Testaments. They serve as reminders of what the reader has read or experienced in the past and serve as a call to practice compassionate justice in the present. The less fortunate in society, including the immigrant, are singled out for care in the Pentateuch. The immigrants are not simply people traveling through the community but are those who have settled down in the community. In Israelite society they would be without any land and means of making a living, so they would be at the mercy of the inhabitants of the land. Thus, a relationship is established between the Israelites and the immigrants. The Israelites are to treat the immigrants with fairness, compassion, and as fellow citizens. The reason for this emerges out of God's own gracious acts toward Israel in delivering them out of being immigrants in Egypt.

The immigrant and the biblical migrant narratives have direct implications for today. The injunction to do the immigrant no harm, to treat him or her as a citizen and to love him or her as one's self is still important. For Milgrom such passages apply directly to present day Israel in how it responds to the Israeli Arabs. "They have thrown in their lot with the Jews of Israel, and according to recent polls, even if a Palestinian state is

---

30. See Exod 1:8–10 concerning the Pharaoh's concern over the rising Hebrew population.

31. See Matt 5:43–48. Quoting Lev 19:18, Jesus extends love from not just one's neighbor but also one's enemy.

formed on Israel's borders, they are determined to remain loyal citizens of the State of Israel."[32]

In light of the terrorist attack on September 11, 2001, the United States has had to reconsider its treatment of citizen and immigrant populations. For the sake of national security, individuals have been jailed with little or no civil rights afforded them based on alleged ties to terrorist organizations. Also, hate crimes against foreign born residents have also increased, especially those of Middle Eastern descent. People must ensure that all are protected and afforded the rights granted citizens by the laws of the land. This includes the natural born citizen, the naturalized immigrant and even the undocumented immigrant.[33] This involves risks in a dangerous world.[34] However, in the effort to avoid terrorism, we cannot forget that, at present, there are approximately 300 million people in the world who are outside of their homeland, immigrants in foreign lands.[35] The purpose of a vast majority of such immigrants is not violence, but a search for a better life for themselves and their families. The threats to the immigrant are real and include hate crimes, human trafficking and other forms of abuse. Milgrom reminds us that "From the perspective of the Torah, the treatment of the immigrant is fraught with universal consequences. It is the acid test of democracy; it challenges the moral integrity of the human soul."[36]

Appendix

Selected Readings on Immigration Myths and Facts

Ewings, Walter A., et al. *The Criminalization of Immigration in the United States.* American Immigration Council. July 2015. http://immigrationpolicy.org/special-reports/criminalization-immigration-united-states.

32. "The Alien in Your Midst," 48.

33. *Plyler v. Doe* 457 U.S. 202 (1982). United States Supreme Court Justice William J. Brennan who gave the Opinion of the Court opinion on Plyler v. Doe (1982) stated: "Whatever his status in the immigration laws, an alien is surely a 'person' in the ordinary sense of that term. Aliens, even aliens whose presence in this country is unlawful, have long been recognized as 'persons' guaranteed due process of law by the Fifth and Fourteenth Amendments." This decision concerned the education of illegal immigrant children in Texas.

34. Hope, "Did I Save Lives or Engage in Profiling?" 12. This article details the quandary one had in taking risks.

35. http://www.amnesty.org/en/refugees-and-migrants.

36. "The Alien in Your Midst," 48.

"5 Facts about Illegal Immigration in the U.S." Pew Research Center. November 19, 2015. http://www.pewresearch.org/fact-tank/2015/11/19/5-facts-about-illegal-immigration-in-the-u-s.

Hunt, Albert R. "Facing the Facts on Illegal Immigration." *The New York Times*, June 19, 2015. http://www.nytimes.com/2015/07/20/us/politics/facing-the-facts-on-illegal-immigration.html?_r=0.

"Immigration Enforcement: FY 2015 ICE Immigration Removals." ICE. https://www.ice.gov/removals-statistics

"New Americans in Kentucky: The Political and Economic Power of Immigrants, Latinos, and Asians in the Bluegrass State." American Immigration Council. March 2015. http://www.immigrationpolicy.org/just-facts/new-americans-kentucky

Smith, S. E. "The Seven Most Dangerous Lies Americans Believe about Immigrants." *The Daily Dot.* May 26, 2015. https://www.google.com/webhp?sourceid=chrome-instant&ion=1&espv=2&ie=UTF-8#q=The+Seven+Most+Dangerous+Lies+Americans+Believe+about+Immigrants.

"SNAP Policy on Non-Citizen Eligibility." http://www.fns.usda.gov/snap/snap-policy-non-citizen-eligibility.

Springford, John. "Is Immigration a Reason for Britain to Leave the EU?" Centre for European Reform. October 2013. https://www.cer.org.uk/sites/default/files/publications/attachments/pdf/2013/pb_imm_uk 27sept13–7892.pdf.

7

Turning Cheeks at Checkpoints

Matthew 5:38–48 as a Text of Terror or Expression of Encouragement for Immigrant Audiences?

—MELANIE A. HOWARD

Introduction

Teaching at Fresno Pacific University, a Hispanic Serving Institution (HSI) in California's Central Valley, means that concerns about immigration and immigrant rights are never far from my mind. Moreover, these questions reflect the lived reality of many of my students who are first- or second-generation immigrants. Thus, I was not surprised when I received the following e-mail from Juan,[1] a student in one of my New Testament courses:

> Tomorrow there will be a community action event at town hall revolving around the issue of our Mayor announcing that our city will not become a sanctuary city. This is an issue that I'm extremely passionate about, and I would love to attend this event. Would you excuse me from class in order to attend this event?

Although the student's request did not surprise me, it deeply touched me, and I responded by observing that his decision to stand with vulnerable and marginalized populations was a perfect object lesson for our class's

---

1 Name changed.

study of the first verses of Matthew's Sermon on the Mount as Jesus identifies vulnerable and marginalized populations in the Beatitudes who are the subject of divine blessing. My exchange with this student was a powerful reminder that teaching about Jesus in the classroom cannot take place apart from attending to the very populations about whom Jesus had the most to say: the poor, the disenfranchised, and the oppressed.

The 2016 presidential election cycle and its aftermath brought questions about immigration both to the national stage and to my classroom. The day after the election, a Latino student e-mailed to inform me that while he would be in class, he would appreciate some grace in his expected participation because of how deeply troubled he was by the results of the election. While he did not specify whether this anxiety was due to concerns about his own documentation status, other conversations around our campus reflected these questions. Thus, in a setting where inquiring about immigration reform and refugee crises is a part of popular discourse, there is an opportunity for new questions to be raised about commonplace beliefs and canonical texts. It is fitting, then, to inquire how the biblical text sounds to immigrant ears, especially Christian immigrants for whom this text is sacred Scripture.[2]

One potentially problematic passage from an immigrant vantage point is the collection of directives urging nonresistance to abuse and love of one's enemies (Matt 5:38–48). Situated in the larger context of the Sermon on the Mount (Matt 5–7), these commands could seem to be

2. For the purposes of this essay, I use the term "immigrant" quite broadly to indicate any individual who has relocated to the United States from any other country, for any reason. Obviously, this entails some broad generalizations. For example, a single, middle-aged, male refugee from Syria would experience the process of immigration differently than a young mother with children from Mexico. These differences should not be overlooked. However, insofar as modern political discourse does not always distinguish among different immigrant communities, I will speak in general terms here about elements of immigrant experiences that might be shared among several immigrant demographics, recognizing that such generalization cannot capture the complexities and difficulties faced by many different immigrant communities. Future work could explore the ways in which particular immigrant demographics experience the biblical text differently. Nonetheless, I am particularly interested here in immigrants who identify as Christian. For the purposes of this essay, I am defining "Christian" as an individual who adheres to the religion associated with the life and teachings of Jesus of Nazareth and who accepts the Gospel of Matthew as a canonical scriptural text. One who reads the Sermon on the Mount as a part of her own religious text will experience it differently than a reader for whom it does not function as Scripture. Thus, while this is not be exclusionary of non-Christian immigrants, it is to suggest that there will likely be more at stake for a Christian immigrant reading this text than for his non-Christian counterpart.

encouraging Christian immigrants to accept with passive acquiescence politicians' threats to build walls and to deport undocumented immigrants. Thus, in a time of intense political debate and in a system that threatens deportation, we might inquire how Matt 5:38–48 sounds to immigrants, especially Christian immigrants who are vulnerable because of their documentation status or their position as victims of acerbic rhetoric. This essay explores two possibilities for interpreting this text: as a text of terror or as a message promising hope within a larger community.

One option for answering the question of how Matt 5:38–48 might sound to immigrant ears is to assert that this text may be a text of terror, that is, a text that includes terrorizing elements or violence inflicted upon its characters and/or its readers. To readers who feel powerless and marginalized, a call to willingly accept further abuse may not be comforting.

Nonetheless, despite the possibility that this text could sound like a text of terror, there may also be notes of hope here. Insofar as a shift in the Greek grammar may allow for the possibility of imagining a larger community, we might still recognize here a message that urges the founding of one's identity in relationship to the community and to the divine.

These possibilities both offer contributions as interpretive paradigms, and both have their own strengths and drawbacks. Because Christian immigrant experiences are necessarily diverse and complex, either (or both!) of these interpretive paradigms could function as a meaningful way for Christian immigrants to interact with the text of Matt 5:38–48. By offering two different interpretive paradigms, then, I am recognizing that diverse audiences will likely include readers for whom either one of these paradigms may resonate more strongly than the other.

This observation gives rise to the need for a word of caution. Although either of these paradigms could reflect some Christian immigrant experiences of the Sermon on the Mount, the task of inquiring about the perspective of any marginalized group is a fraught one. I must be clear, then, that I am not attempting to provide a voice to all, or even *any*, Christian immigrant readers. My attempt here is not to speak for other audiences or to be either prescriptive or descriptive of the task of reading Matt 5:38–48 from a marginalized Christian immigrant perspective. Rather, this study is an attempt to offer exegetical and hermeneutical explorations of a biblical text that could resonate particularly with Christian immigrant audiences generally, and perhaps even with students like Juan with whom I have the privilege of interacting every day. My hope is that the reading paradigms offered here would help my students discover a language for articulating their own experiences of this text. As such, the object of study here is not a people group but a text, and this essay is an effort to identify several ways in which that text might function for a diverse, yet marginalized, community for whom it functions as sacred Scripture.

The Sermon as a Text of Terror for Christian Immigrant Audiences[3]

Naming any part of scripture a "text of terror" could seem like a drastic step. Nonetheless, some marginalized immigrant audiences may recognize elements of the text that put them personally at risk when read in the context of the present day social and political environment of the United States. In this sense, the Sermon on the Mount, especially its commands to nonresistance and love of enemy (5:38–48), might be a text of terror for immigrants today.

The phrase "text of terror" is, perhaps, most famously associated with Phyllis Trible's early use of the expression to describe texts in the (Hebrew) Bible that portray women as the victims of heinous abuses.[4] Trible maintains that her reading of tales such as the rejection of Hagar (Gen 21:8–21), the rape of Tamar (2 Sam 13:1–22), and the slaughter of Jephthah's daughter (Judg 11:29–40) "interprets stories of outrage on behalf of their female victims in order to recover a neglected history, to remember a past that the present embodies, and to pray that these terrors shall not come to pass again."[5] By Trible's definition, then, the "text of terror" genre is constituted primarily by terrorizing elements internal to the text.

While Trible's task is primarily a literary one insofar as she lends a sympathetic eye to the female characters of the particular tales that she examines, her reading nonetheless opens the door for similar readings of Scripture that are able to identify particularly problematic passages as "texts of terror." That is, "text of terror" as a category need not be limited to only narrative texts where characters internal to the text itself are terrorized. Indeed, poetic texts like Ps 137:9 promising the dashing of babies against rocks is surely a "text of terror," even if it does not contain literary characters as

---

3 I have explored this concept in a previously published article that explored reading this passage in Matthew as satire, as an imperative for peace-making, and as a text of terror (Howard, "Paradigm of Peace, Silly Satire, Text of Terror," 110–46).

4 Trible, *Texts of Terror*.

5 Trible, *Texts of Terror*, 3.

such who are the victims of that terror. Thus, the "text of terror" category is malleable enough to include even texts whose victims are external modern readers and not only internal literary characters. Indeed, several scholars since Trible have also taken up her language and applied it to both narrative and non-narrative (e.g. poetic, didactic, eschatological) texts that make victims of external readers, not only internal characters.[6]

While the reading of the Sermon on the Mount offered here is inspired by Trible's project and method, it is by no means limited to these. Where Trible offers a sympathetic reading of literary characters in the Hebrew Bible, the reading of the Sermon on the Mount here instead presents a sympathetic reading of Jesus's own words, asking how these words might form a "text of terror" for a different audience: present-day Christian immigrants. Trible identifies "texts of terror" as passages that recount tales where women are victims. However, victims need not be confined to the pages of Scripture. Rather, Scripture can create its own victims in modern times. Thus, one might argue that the Sermon on the Mount, and particularly its imperatives of nonresistance and love of enemies in Matt 5:38–48, can be classified as a "text of terror" from the perspective of Christian immigrant audiences.

One way in which Matt 5:38–48 can become a text of terror for Christian immigrant audiences is in its juxtaposition of "neighbor" not with "foreigner," but with "enemy" (5:43). Jesus's teaching here is one of several antitheses that punctuate the first part of the Sermon on the Mount (cf. 5:21–22, 27–28, 31–32, 33–34, 38–39). In the antitheses, the Matthean Jesus quotes a command from the Torah and then expounds on that law with a teaching that appears to offer a heightened ethic.

The antithesis in 5:43–44 is a rather peculiar one for several reasons. First, Jesus's quotation from Lev 19:18 is quite selective. The larger

---

6 Cf., e.g., Dillen, "Good News for Children?," 164–82; Neville, "Toward a Hermeneutic of Shalom," 339–48; Rogers, "Texts of Terror," 205–12. In his reading of the book of Judges, John Thompson defines the "text of terror" category almost solely in relation to the texts' readers. Thompson names the "text of terror" category as comprising "texts in the Bible that have the potential to evoke from thoughtful readers a response that is appropriately described as terror" ("Preaching Texts of Terror in the Book of Judges," 49). Though some scholars who work with the "text of terror" category are not always as explicit as Thompson in defining the category vis-à-vis the text's readers, Thompson articulates a tendency that is nonetheless observable in the work of many who have taken up Trible's language, even without adopting her limitation of defining terror only in relation to the characters within a narrative. Here, I am following Thompson in identifying passages as "texts of terror" on the basis of the texts' ability to evoke a response of terror in the audience.

commandment in Leviticus instructs, "You shall love your neighbor as yourself: I am the LORD."[7] Second, the "quotation" includes text ("and hate your enemy") that does not appear in Lev 19:18. Each of these oddities merits consideration.

First, it is notable that the quotation of Lev 19:18 leaves out the text in Leviticus immediately following Jesus's selection. Both the qualifier "as yourself" and the statement "I am the LORD" are absent from the Matthean text. The omission of "I am the LORD" could be explained by the narrative awkwardness that would have resulted for the evangelist by placing these words in Jesus's mouth.[8] On the absence of "as yourself," Hans Deiter Betz speculates that the "words 'as yourself' imply a positive valuation of self-love. Such an emphasis on self-love, however, appears to be improper in a context where the doctrine of the imitation of God is the guiding doctrine."[9] That is, the driving force of Jesus's teaching in Matt 5:43–48 might be summarized most simply not as "love your enemies" (Matt 5:44), but rather as "be like God" (cf. Matt 5:48).[10] Thus, Matthew's omission of these portions of the text in Leviticus are understandable.

However, the absence of Levitical text from Matt 5:43 is only one piece of this quotation's oddities. The other peculiarity worth noting is the addition of the phrase "and hate your enemy," which is not found in Lev 19:18. Although this phrase is not in Leviticus, the *Community Rule* from Qumran includes language about hating those who are outside of the community's boundaries.[11] This suggests to some that Matthew's text has been influenced by the Qumran community or perhaps other forms of ancient Judaism that

7 Translation from the NRSV.

8. Nonetheless, the meaning of the quotation from Leviticus may change slightly with the omission of this final phrase. As Pinchas Lapide observes, "If love of neighbor is not to degenerate into a surely horizontal making use of others . . . it needs a supplement: I am (God) the Lord. For only under the common fatherhood of God does love of neighbor have meaning and significance as fellowship" (*Sermon on the Mount*, 78). Though offering a harsher formulation than Betz, Lapide shares in a comparable conclusion: in the Sermon on the Mount, ethics is properly grounded only in the imitation of God.

9 Betz, *Sermon on the Mount*, 303.

10 Robert Guelich, taking a more dismissive approach, simply contends, "This omission doubtless resulted from the conjunction of the two commands in 5:43a, b, and does not affect the import of the commandment" (*The Sermon on the Mount*, 225). Regardless of whether this omission was theologically relevant (so Betz) or merely the result of stylistic considerations (so Guelich), the absence of the phrase is nonetheless noteworthy.

11 See 1QS 1:4 which reads, in part, "that they may love all that He has chosen and hate all that he has rejected" (translation from Vermes, *Complete Dead Sea Scrolls*, 98).

adopted similar mentalities toward outsiders.[12] While it would be difficult to prove a genetic relationship between the Dead Sea Scrolls and the Gospel of Matthew, the presence of a similar sentiment in the Scrolls could suggest that it represents a popular mindset in Jesus's (and/or Matthew's) day.

For modern-day Christian immigrant audiences, the addition of the phrase "hate your enemy" could suggest that this is a text of terror. As noted above, the "neighbor" in the first part of 5:43 is contrasted not with "foreigner," but with enemy. Thus, because one might imagine that "foreigner" is the natural antithesis of "neighbor," the inclusion of "enemy" here could suggest a subtle conflation of "foreigner" with "enemy." By this reading, immigrant audiences may be troubled by the question of whether this biblical text is naming them an "enemy" to be hated.

To be sure, the biblical text never directly correlates foreigners with enemies. However, there are several places outside of Matthew where foreigners are depicted as acting in a threatening or malicious manner. Throughout the Hebrew Bible, the text makes use of the term *nokrî* to discuss certain foreigners. Unlike other foreigners (identified as *ge*[set macron over e]*rim*), the *nokrîm* are frequently portrayed as possessing malicious qualities. At the very least, such foreigners are described as second-rate individuals, and the contrast between them and the *ge*[set macron over e]*rim* is most evident in Deut 14:21. In that text, the Israelites are instructed not to eat anything that dies of natural causes. In the case that they should acquire such meat, they are given two options: simply giving it away freely to a *ge*[set macron over e]*r* or selling it for a cost to a *nokrî*. That is, individuals who are *nokrîm* are not to be granted the same access to free food as other foreigners.[13]

Beyond simply being classed as inferior individuals, the *nokrîm* of the Hebrew Bible are also characterized as a corrupting influence capable of producing disastrous consequences for Israel's faithful ones. Foreign women, the *nokrîyôt*, are particularly dangerous in this regard. Their harmful influence distracts Solomon (1 Kgs 11:1), and both Ezra and Nehemiah are anxious to rid the assembly of their presence (Ezra 10:6–44; Neh 13:23–31).

---

12 See Schlabach, "'Confessional' Nonviolence and the Unity of the Church," 132. W. D. Davies posits that, in fact, Matt 5:43–48 is Jesus's criticism of the Qumran sectarians such that Jesus's instructions here are intended as a direct counterpoint to the teachings of that community (*Sermon on the Mount*, 140–41; cf. Betz, *Sermon on the Mount*, 304).

13. Additionally, the *nokrîm* described in Gen 31:15 and Deut 23:20 appear as "second-class" citizens who, if not actively oppressed, are clearly demeaned in the social hierarchy. Furthermore, Isa 2:6 seems to imagine the *nokrîm* as a negative influence.

Furthermore, Proverbs issues frequent warnings about the *nokrîyah* whose seduction might distract an otherwise well-intentioned young man (Prov 2:16; 5:20; 6:24; 7:5; 23:27).[14]

The *nokrîm* are further characterized as suspicious individuals because of their propensity for taking what is not rightfully their own. They will take one's wealth (Prov 5:10), one's inheritance (Lam 5:2), and even one's land (Obad 1:11). Thus, even if these foreigners are not explicitly identified as "enemies," their deeds are consonant with adversarial actions such that "foreigner" is not so different from "enemy," especially if that foreigner is a *nokrî*.

Given the possible conflation of "foreigner" and "enemy" within the Hebrew Bible, it is not a stretch to imagine a similar conflation within Matthew, whether in the author's own mind or in the minds of modern audiences. Thus, the phrase "hate your enemy" in Matt 5:43 may make this text sound like a text of terror to Christian immigrant audiences who hear a similar correspondence between "foreigner" and "enemy."

Indeed, a connection between "foreigner" and "enemy" may not be so absurd given the contemporary political climate of the United States. As Patricia Ehrkamp and Caroline Nagel observe, "The devolution of immigration policy in the United States has expanded border control and immigration policing from the external border to include interior spaces of the United States and has rendered the lives of immigrants—especially undocumented immigrants—increasingly precarious."[15] As this policing of immigrants moves away from geographical boundary markers and turns toward immigrant residents, immigrants who hear the Sermon's apposition of "neighbor" and "enemy" might be reminded of the unsafe spaces that they occupy, whether in or beyond borderlands.

In this sort of political environment, polarizing rhetoric can feel especially dangerous, and it can increase listeners' sensitivity to such language even beyond the sphere of politics. Without this contemporary political context, some readers may not detect any threatening elements within the Sermon on the Mount. However, in a context where political rhetoric has linked immigrants to enemies, some readers may become uneasy at the potentially

14 Although the Hebrew text of Proverbs uses the term *nokrîyah* to identify this foreign woman, several English translations opt for terms that characterize this figure in terms of unrestrained sexual behavior. For example, in Prov 2:16 she is identified alternatively as "the wayward woman" (NIV), "the promiscuous woman" (NLT), "the adulteress" (ESV, NRSV, NASB), or "the immoral woman" (ISV).

15 Ehrkamp and Nagel, "'Under the Radar,'" 319.

polarizing language that can be found within the biblical text. Thus, the polarization of "neighbor" and "enemy" language in the text of Matthew may feel more threatening because of the current political context.

Beyond the potential danger of equating "enemy" with "foreigner," Matt 5:43 may also appear as a text of terror because of the seemingly clear line that it draws between "neighbor" and "enemy." Such a line suggests a clear differentiation of one's location. However, for some immigrant audiences, life in the borderlands can be far more ambiguous and dangerous. As recently as October 2015, Newsweek exposed the harsh realities that Mexican immigrants face as they attempt to relocate to the United States.[16] The exposé revealed a host of dangers: sexual assault, abandonment, kidnapping, extortion, and even death. In other words, the space between countries is not always clearly marked, and it can be a dangerous territory to occupy. This liminal space can be made to stretch on almost indefinitely when one adds to the list of dangers the possibility of detention at the hands of Homeland Security or ICE agents.

A view of Matt 5:38–48 that recognizes it as a text of terror has much to offer. However, there are admittedly certain drawbacks to this interpretive model as well. First, viewing this passage as a text of terror could seem to be a willful misreading of the text that unfairly identifies terrorizing elements when they are not actually there. That is, readers from this text of terror paradigm might be subject to the critique that such an approach fuses exegetical insights about the text with reader responses to that text. Such a conflation fails, then, to account for the historical, geographical, and cultural distance between the text and the reader.

Second, for marginalized Christian immigrant audiences that approach this text as sacred Scripture, the naming of any biblical text as a "text of terror" could seem to undermine the status of the text as a formative part of the Christian canon. Thus, in an attempt to attend to the experiences of Christian immigrant audiences in one regard by recognizing experiences of uncertainty and fear, this approach could ultimately fail to provide attention to another aspect of the identity of Christian immigrant audiences by diminishing the authority of a text that is deeply cherished.

The text of terror lens offers both positive contributions as well as potential drawbacks for Christian immigrant audiences. While this lens may be better equipped to attend to the particular circumstances of such

16 Eichenwald, "Borderline Insanity."

audiences, it may ultimately sacrifice some attention to the text itself and other aspects of immigrants' identities in doing so.

Finding Encouragement and Hope in the Sermon on the Mount

Identifying Matt 5:38–48 as a text of terror for immigrant populations could give the impression that redeeming this passage for and with such audiences is a hopeless endeavor. However, without minimizing the real potential for this text to be problematic, we might nonetheless detect at least a hint of hope. This intimation comes in the form of an unexpected change in the method of address from second person singular to second person plural in the Greek text of this passage.

The pericope begins largely by using the second person singular. Verse 39, though beginning with a command to "y'all" (ὑμιν, *humin*) to practice nonresistance, shifts to provide an example in the singular: "whoever strikes you (singular) . . ." The use of the singular is sustained in the verses that follow as Jesus gives the examples of offering one's cloak when sued for a coat (v. 40), walking two miles when compelled for one (v. 41), and giving to the one who asks (v. 42). Finally, the second person singular appears in the quotation of Lev 19:18 at the beginning of verse 43 in the instruction to love one's neighbor.

These uses of the second person singular are contrasted with the use of the second person plural, especially later in the pericope. Like verse 39, verse 43 introduces its subject matter to the plural audience: "Y'all (ὑμιν, *humin*) have heard it said . . ." This is interrupted by the second person singular in the quotation from Leviticus, but Jesus returns to the plural in verses 44–48 on the subject of loving enemies. Where verses 39–42 assume situations in which an individual is the victim of various abuses, verses 44–48 posit a larger community that is encountering opposition. That is, opposition is moved from the context of a conflict between persons to a struggle between communities.

It may seem that such a small grammatical change could hardly serve as the basis for reading this text as a source of hope for immigrant audiences given the possibility for Matt 5:38–48 to be a text of terror.[17] Nonetheless, I would suggest that it may be that the general move from the use of the second

---

17 Indeed, I want to cautious *not* to suggest that the interpretation that I am offering here simply erases every possibility for this text to be problematic for immigrant audiences.

person singular to the second person plural could offer a hopeful message about the location of personal identity not in oneself, but in relation to one's larger community and, ultimately, in relation to God (cf. 5:45).

The second part of this pericope begins in verse 43 with a quotation of the Septuagint's translation of Lev 19:18 in which the relationship with one's neighbor is imagined on an individual level insofar as the Levitical text urges love of your (singular) neighbor. However, as Jesus interprets this text in the verses that follow, it quickly becomes apparent that he is imagining larger webs of connection insofar as every second person verb and pronoun from verses 44–48 is plural. This shift, then, has the effect of moving the locus of identity away from the individual and toward the communal.

Even beyond a move from individual to communal, verses 44–48 offer a foundation for identity that extends beyond the human community. The rationale for extending love to enemies is so that "y'all" would be children of the father in heaven (v. 45). Similarly, the pericope concludes with an imperative to be perfect due to the heavenly father's own perfection (v. 48). Thus, the text seems to suggest that the grounding for all of these instructions is one's connection with the heavenly father.

By locating identity beyond the human realm, Jesus implicitly offers immigrant audiences a source of hope and empowerment. That is, this text may suggest that if one's identity is ultimately founded on the basis of a relationship to the divine, then human governments that threaten deportation may seem to pose less of a threat. Such an interpretation recalls Jesus's teaching elsewhere in Matthew where he offers the advice, "Do not fear those who kill the body but cannot kill the soul" (10:28). Love for any human enemy, then, is possible because such an enemy is incapable of killing the soul. Thus, immigrant audiences reading 5:38–48 may be able to reimagine their identity both in communal and divine terms. In doing this, such audiences might find some comfort, even in the midst of otherwise dangerous and terrifying situations.

In many ways, this establishment of identity in a community, even in the midst of dangerous times, is precisely what my student Juan was doing as he joined others to protest our city's refusal to become a sanctuary city. Although he may not have articulated it in such terms, Juan was recognizing that by joining his brothers and sisters on the picket line, he was a member of a community both within and opposed to the geopolitical powers around him. Though positioned in the politically dangerous situation of overtly opposing public policy, Juan was finding comfort and support in the community of activists and immigrants whom he joined.

The move from the individual to the communal in Matt 5:38–48 not only provides a subtle message of hope for immigrant audiences, but it also provides a subtle imperative for non-immigrant audiences.[18] That is, insofar as non-immigrant Christian audiences are willing to hear this text's call to action, Jesus's words here issue an implicit demand for advocacy. If this text is to offer the hope that identity and support can be found in a community, then it becomes the responsibility of the text's readers to provide that community to other readers. Being perfect "as your heavenly Father is perfect" (5:48) entails providing a supportive community for those whom the Beatitudes name as blessed. Thus, this text contains both a note of hope for Christian immigrant audiences and a word of instruction, perhaps especially for other Christian audiences composed of non-immigrants.

Terrorizing Text or Hope for Healing?

Arguably, a preacher's primary task is to proclaim the Bible's Good News to a particular gathering of God's people. What, then, is the good news of Matt 5:38–48 for immigrant audiences? As this essay has shown, there is not an easy answer to this question. On the one hand, viewing this passage as a text of terror that threatens the safety of some audiences is a viable option. On the other hand, there is the possibility that this text might offer a glimmer of hope to hurting audiences and a promise of Good News found in the context of relationships within communities and with the divine.

It is, perhaps, tempting to jump to this latter option (the text as a word of hope) as the place where one encounters the Gospel in this text. However, to look only at this final option is to overlook the potential contributions of a text of terror viewpoint. Both interpretive paradigms offer suggestions for how this single text might function for the diverse and complex communities of marginalized Christian immigrants for whom the Sermon on the Mount is Scripture. When we view the Sermon through the text of terror paradigm, we are equipped to detect the ways in which this text might contain echoes of the dangerous and polarizing political rhetoric about immigration. When viewed as a potential message of hope, this text might be

18 I am grateful to participants in the 2016 "Bible and Practical Theology" session at the annual meeting of the Society for Biblical Literature who suggested this point in response to an earlier version of this paper that was delivered there.

able to offer comfort and encouragement to immigrant Christian audiences who feel isolated or anxious.

Nonetheless, there is no one immigrant experience. Even when we focus primarily on Christian immigrants who are particularly vulnerable, it is still impossible to capture every aspect of this social location. Given this diversity, then, it is helpful to consider a multiplicity of options for how some immigrant communities might encounter the Sermon on the Mount, especially in its instructions regarding nonresistance and enemy love. While the possibilities offered here are certainly not exhaustive, they may nonetheless highlight the spectrum of ways in which the Sermon on the Mount can interact with Christian immigrant communities today.

I find myself wondering how Juan, the student who requested permission to miss class in order to advocate for undocumented immigrants, would respond to this text. Although he did not offer a comment on this particular pericope when we studied it in class, he did come to my office a few weeks after the rally to tell me about his experience at the event. In our conversation, he shared with me his desire to devote his future career to public policy work so that he could continue to advocate for marginalized populations.

The class that Juan took with me will likely be his only encounter with academic biblical studies, but my hope is that he will have glimpsed the possibilities for how Jesus's teachings can inform the work that he will do. Although I was unable to join Juan on the picket lines as he demonstrated his support for immigrants in our city, his actions have inspired me to consider how my own work as a biblical scholar might support his cause. So, it is for Juan, and for so many others like him, that I offer these readings of Matt 5:38–48. My hope is that with these exegetical and hermeneutical tools in hand, he will be better equipped to serve the communities to which he belongs and with whom he serves.

8

Moving from Caution to Faithful Proclamation

One Pastor's Story

—Owen K Ross

Introduction

"If someone asks you about immigration, treat it like you are Teflon. Don't let the question stick. Let the question just slide and keep going," I advised the seminary intern as he was going to speak to a Sunday school class at one of the supporting churches of the mission I pastored. I was afraid to jeopardize funding by engaging in politics. Christ's Foundry United Methodist Mission was founded as a holistic mission of the North Texas Conference of The United Methodist Church in 2002. The mission field was and is located in the Latin American immigrant neighborhood located just north of Love Field in Dallas, Texas. I knew that ministry in this setting with a low-income community would be dependent on outside funding for many years, so I was hesitant to address issues of immigration for fear of offending donors.

Immigration and border issues are contentious political topics. Passions abound on all sides of the issues. My belief at the time was that taking a position on such a contentious political issue would jeopardize the funding of this emerging ministry in a low-income community. Avoidance was the policy for the first couple of years, until I became more familiar with the community and until I better discerned what the Bible has to say about immigration.

I understand why so many preachers avoid preaching on immigration. However, a preacher must act intentionally to *avoid* texts in the Bible that relate directly to immigration. No other contemporary political issue is more directly, frequently, and consistently addressed in Scripture than immigration. Many preachers treat texts relating to immigration like my six-year-old son often treats cracks in an old, busted sidewalk when he is in a playful mood. My son performs skillful steps to avoid the cracks, just as many preachers skillfully avoid preaching on texts that speak directly to issues of immigration. To avoid the subject takes intentionality and is unfaithful to Scripture.

This chapter equips preachers to stand fast to Scripture when teaching or preaching about immigration or border issues. This chapter shares ideas for how preachers can exegete texts to assist their listeners to think about immigration and border issues in light of Scripture. This chapter will also share my journey from avoiding issues relating to immigration when speaking to potential donors to becoming the pastor of the first congregation in North Texas to publicly proclaim itself to be a new sanctuary church. Finally, this chapter will share some ways to approach issues of immigration at specific times of the year. My prayer is that preachers who read this chapter will not only become emboldened to preach frequently on this topic in their contexts but also find the resources to navigate the challenging path of effectively preaching on what can be a very contentious issue in a preacher's congregation.

Immigration Is not a New Issue

Since Adam and Eve left the garden of Eden, humans across the globe have been on the move. People have crossed all types of physical and political borders. Scripture documents some of these movements. Abraham was called to leave the land of his ancestors (Gen 12). God called Jacob to move his family to Egypt (Gen 46). The Israelites frequently were referred to as foreigners while they were in Egypt (Exod 22:21; Lev 19:34; Deut 10:19). Moses was a stranger in Midian (Acts 7:29). The book of Exodus documents God's people moving towards the Promised Land to establish their own nation. The Holy Family moved from Bethlehem to Egypt and then to Nazareth (Matt 2). The book of Acts recounts Paul's travels.

This migration that began with Adam and Eve leaving the garden continues today. Economic hardship, pursuit of freedom, escape from persecution or famine, disasters, family unification, and other forces push and pull persons to cross borders around the globe. People are free to cross some of these borders, like state borders in the United States or national borders within certain unions. Other borders have greater restrictions depending on the laws of each nation. Some persons are exempt from those restrictions and come into those countries through proper channels. Others would be stopped by those restrictions and enter through illegal means. Other times, persons enter through legal means but overstay the time allowed. Others enter through legal means, but persons charged with executing, interpreting, or enforcing laws deem such persons as living in the country illegally. While there is much complexity to immigration and border issues, God's Word consistently teaches how individuals and nations must treat foreigners.

Many of the issues that persons and nations face today did not exist in biblical times and as such, are not directly addressed in Scripture. For those issues *not* directly addressed in Scripture, preachers must take nuanced approaches to texts and themes in Scripture to draw wisdom in preaching on such issues. Immigration does not fall into this category. Again, *no other contemporary political issue is more directly, frequently, and consistently addressed in Scripture than immigration.* Immigration was an issue in biblical times as immigration is an issue today. Therefore, in biblical times as well as in our contemporary world, the people of God need God's wisdom in responding to the presence of foreigners in their societies.

The reason immigration is so frequently addressed in Scripture is that the people of Israel were forming a nation. Their nation and their cities would have borders. Foreigners lived within some of these borders, and foreigners also immigrated to within Israel's borders. As such, the people of Israel would face the same issue that every nation faces. How should we respond to the foreigner living among us or arriving to or within our borders?

God assisted the people of Israel and now assists those who seek God's will today through direct guidance. God bluntly instructed the people of Israel as they sought to form their nation to avoid becoming like other nations, "Do not mistreat or oppress an alien, for you were aliens in Egypt" (Exod 22:21 NIV. All quotes in this chapter are from the NIV. The term that the NIV translates as "alien" can better be understood as "foreigner" or "sojourner."). God repeats the instruction in Exod 23:9 and Lev 19:33. The prophets reminded God's people of these instructions (Jer 22:3; Zech 7:10; Mal 3:5). In these instructions, God never makes any distinction of legal status among these sojourners, migrants, immigrants, or foreigners in how they are to be treated. God clearly and repeatedly established that those considered foreigners, regardless of status or origins, *should NOT be mistreated.*

God's instructions went beyond the basic duty of *not* mistreating and *not* oppressing foreigners. God codified the *duty to care* for foreigners. The law instructed landowners to leave the grapes that had fallen, the gleanings, and the harvest at the edges of the fields for the poor and the foreigner (Lev 19:10; 23:22; and Deut 24:17–21). Even a part of *the tithe* was to be designated for foreigners (Deut 14:28–29; 26:12). The prophet Ezekiel would later instruct the Israelites to allot land to foreigners in the same way as native-born Israelites, as an inheritance (Ezek 47:21–23). Indeed, equality between the Israelites and foreigners is a prevalent and consistent theme in Scripture (Exod 23:12; Lev 16:29; 24:22; Num 15:15–16; and many others). Preachers should familiarize their listeners with these texts as many forces in the United States promote double standards between citizens and immigrants, both authorized and unauthorized.

An argument often made by Christians who promote double standards between native-born and foreign-born is that even though Christians have a duty *as individuals* to care for needy immigrants, the collective (the government) is not bound by such duty. I have heard said, "I am not personally withholding justice from or abusing foreigners." Often times an anecdote of volunteering at a food closet or a charity follows to deflect questions of justice. Their eisegesis of Scripture requires a supposition that the law was given not to the nation of Israel but simply as a code of conduct for individuals. Only by mental gymnastics can one believe that these texts are exclusively for individuals and not for the collective. Clearly the law is given to the collective, the government, and individuals that make up the collective.

While I was waffling in my first years in ministry as to how to address the issue of immigration and treating it like Teflon, God had already chosen a side. Scripture clearly establishes God's side in the debate. Deuteronomy 10:18–19 (NIV) states, "He [God] *defends* the cause of the fatherless and the widow, and loves the alien, giving him food and clothing. And you are to love those who are aliens, for you yourselves were aliens in Egypt" (emphasis mine). The Psalmist states, "The Lord watches over the alien and sustains the fatherless and the widow, but he frustrates the ways of the wicked" (Ps 146:9).

While the Psalmist merely suggests the wickedness of those who do not care for foreigners, the Lord in Deuteronomy explicitly states, "Cursed is the man who withholds justice from the alien" (Deut 27:19). Early in my ministry at Christ's Foundry, I *eventually discovered* God's instructions in the law of how God guided the nation of Israel to address the same immigration problems my country faced. On this contemporary debate of how foreigners are to be treated, regardless of their status, God chose a side when Israel engaged in the same debate the United States and others engage today. God has not changed sides. I needed to pick a side, and I became ready to do so when I realized that those who do not defend foreigners *do not* participate on God's side in this historic and contemporary issue.

The Change

After witnessing and experiencing the effects of the draconian immigration policies on the community around Christ's Foundry and after becoming more acquainted with Scripture relating to immigration, I sensed God saying to me, "Owen, you must choose who you will serve. You cannot serve me and money. You must choose." I knew what that meant. I and the staff and people of Christ's Foundry could no longer treat immigration issues like Teflon. We had to choose between serving God and serving money. We chose God.

By 2004, Christ's Foundry had become a leading advocate on issues dealing with immigration in Dallas and in The United Methodist Church. The staff of Christ's Foundry developed a lecture series called, "Jesus Outside the Gates." This series and other lessons on immigration were given at various local United Methodist Churches. I spoke in Sunday school classes, UMW meetings, United Methodist Men's groups, in church gatherings, at Perkins School of Theology, and any other venue where I would receive an invitation. Immigration would work its way into sermons as I was invited to guest preach.

We launched the "WWJD? Who Would Jesus Deport?" campaign. We designed T-shirts and bumper stickers. I bought the website www.WhoWouldJesusDeport.com, which evolved over the years, and today, includes a list of scriptures that address the issue of immigration.

After my conviction in the first two years of serving Christ's Foundry through greater exposure to the Bible and to the reality of the undocumented immigrant in the U.S., the staff and members of Christ's Foundry and I began connecting with community organizing groups and engaging in activism. Christ's Foundry hosted many of these groups seeking a place to meet. Leaders in Christ's Foundry and I became prominent in the local community organizing groups.

By 2009, Christ's Foundry was worshipping a little over 100 persons, the majority of adults being unauthorized residents. The congregation had gained the reputation as a leader in immigration reform, and I had become emboldened to be a more public advocate and organizer. As a result, advocacy and community organizing groups called upon me to speak and to give the invocations or benedictions at actions, meetings, and marches. The congregation participated in actions and over the years had collaborated with most of the community organizing entities in the DFW area.

On March 21, 2010, Christ's Foundry organized two full fifty-passenger busses that included fifty Christ's Foundry members to participate in the March for America to call for comprehensive immigration reform in Washington, DC. Our organizing work was featured nationally on Fox News and received significant local coverage. With this action as well as the continued partnership with the advocate and community organizing entities, Christ's Foundry could no longer hide its public positions on immigration, because it had emerged as a sought-after leader on issues on immigration.

Occasionally, the pastors of supporting churches or I would receive complaints. I received negative comments on social media as well as a few nasty phone calls. However, my fears of losing financial support that had caused my earlier unfaithfulness in responding to immigration issues never materialized. I sought to be faithful to God and found God to be faithful. Not only did Christ's Foundry never finish a year in debt after 2005, Christ's Foundry also built a $2.5 million facility in 2011 that was debt-free by September 2012. Then, by my last year at the church in 2017, Christ's Foundry had grown to be the largest Spanish-language congregation in United Methodism. God was and is faithful and calls us to faithfulness.

Standing Fast to Scripture

When I preached on immigration in the Christ's Foundry congregation, I was not taking a boldly prophetic stand. I was preaching to the choir. Only when I accepted invitations to teach, preach, or speak on immigration in settings that included many who voted contrary to the wellbeing of unauthorized immigrants was I being bold or truly prophetic. I accomplished this by standing fast to Scripture, avoiding partisanship, and following the techniques I share in this chapter.

Preachers face a justifiable fear of preaching excessively political sermons, but too many preachers slip from preaching faithful, *political sermons* into preaching unfaithful, *partisan sermons*. Preachers should recognize the temptation of misusing the pulpit as a medium to promote the platform of his or her preferred political party. Sermons can address political topics without slipping into partisanship.

Avoiding the topic of immigration or other contentious political issues in sermons and in listeners is understandable. It can be scary. It can go very badly. Persons can and will misinterpret what you are saying as well as the point of the sermon. Therefore, preaching on contentious political issues, especially in diverse or opposing settings takes skill, preparation, and humility. While preachers *should* avoid being *too* political and partisan, becoming aware of when a preacher is crossing the line from being faithful and prophetic into misusing one's authority and misusing Scripture in addressing political issue takes wisdom and humility.

The temptation to practice eisegesis (imposing one's own bias on Scripture in order to utilize Scripture to justify one's own agenda) instead of exegesis (seeking to draw out the meaning of the Scripture) happens in every sermon. The temptation to eisegete arises particularly in sermons that address political issues. When preachers slip into becoming propagandists for political parties, we lose our prophetic voices.

Therefore, preachers must be equal opportunity offenders when addressing political issues. They must stand fast to the tenants of the faith to avoid the temptation to yield to political influences that can often times be tied to dollars. We face the tempting diversion of pointing fingers and casting stones at preachers who obviously and habitually do this on television. I encourage the pastors first to evaluate themselves, for all preachers confront the temptation to eisegete. However, do not let the fear of eisegeting texts when addressing contemporary political issues cause you to avoid contemporary political issues.

The most effective lesson I developed on immigration could be adapted for sermons but is designed for group discussion. The lesson begins by sharing a long list of over twenty-five texts related to immigration. Ideally, each person in the audience would have the texts in their hands. This chapter addresses most of these texts, and the actual list of texts appears at my website www.WhoWouldJesusDeport.com. After putting the list of texts in the hands of the audience, I would highlight various texts from the Law, Psalms, Prophets, Gospels, and Paul's writings, similar to how I present these texts in this chapter.

After this survey of Scripture relating to immigration with a few personal stories of how these texts relate to contemporary immigration activities and enforcement in the United States, I would pose the question, "If the United States of America were a Christian nation . . . " I would pause here as such a statement generally caught the attention of the audience. I would then clarify, "Not a democracy as we are, but a Christian theocracy with our laws based primarily if not exclusively on the Bible, what would our immigration policy look like?" I would then pause and wait for a response from the audience.

Usually a few persons were quick to share the obvious answers that our laws would express that we love them. Our laws would welcome them and treat them like native-born citizens. Our policies would support their endeavors to seek better lives for themselves and their families. This very simple exercise was the most effective means that I found to engage persons who supported detrimental policies to unauthorized immigrants or politicians who legislated or executed such policies to explore about their stances in light of Scripture. While this presentation was the most effective that I discovered to engage persons in antagonistic contexts, this presentation is also full of pitfalls.

I encourage presenters engaging these ideas not to allow themselves to become defensive or distracted. *Avoid expressing personal opinion on immigration or politicians and political parties in the presentation before the audience reaches consensus about what Scripture says.* This type of presentation seeks to gain a general acknowledgement and consensus from the audience that Scripture teaches individuals and nations to care for foreigners and treat them as native-born. Key is to establish clarity about what Scripture says about immigration *before* addressing how Christians should respond to Scripture's teachings on immigration. Again, and I cannot emphasis this enough, gain consensus on what Scripture says before addressing how to respond.

Generally, some persons who support nativist policies or candidates would want to deflect and talk about the complications from such a policy before directly and clearly responding to the question about Scripture. Other opponents would want to deflect by saying that I was proof texting. I would respond, "It is hard to proof text this many texts. When you have this copious supply of clear and direct verses on any topic, the preacher no longer engages in proof texting, but in identifying clear and dominant themes, messages, and motifs in Holy Scripture." Again, keep the group focused until consensus is gained about what Scripture says, although disagreement will surely exist on the application of the texts.

Opponents would quote other texts that appeared to contradict what the superabundance of texts on the list shared. Without fail, someone will point to Rom 13. Others will point to other texts about God or King David establishing national borders. The purpose of opponents in pointing to these texts is to deflect from examining their own moral behavior by examining the moral behaviors of persons who cross borders without government authorization.

While many political, historical, and humanitarian arguments can be raised to defend persons crossing borders without authorization, one does not study the Bible to equip oneself to identify the sins of others as much as to identify one's own sin and seek forgiveness, correction, and salvation. While I might note that none of the Scriptures on the list suggest doing away with all national borders and while I would feel greatly tempted to defend the reasons people make unauthorized border crossings, my goal was to keep the group focused on the texts and what God had consistently communicated to the people of Israel before engaging what God is communicating to the audience through those texts. I might say, "This lesson would be different if we were all unauthorized immigrants and seeking what Scriptures on immigration were speaking to us, but in acknowledging that the vast majority of us are citizens of this land, let us focus on what Scripture is saying to us."

The presenter must use discipline to keep the topic on how those living in a land where immigrants reside and continue to arrive should respond. In other words, help the group understand that before seeking to remove the specks from the eyes of unauthorized immigrants, the group should explore in light of the list of scriptures the logs that exist in the eyes of the U.S. citizenry (Matt 7:3–5). I found groups would eventually concede that the Bible's teaching on immigration is much more compassionate than current U.S. policy. At that point, I would respond, "Now we understand what God's Word says about the issue, what shall we do with God's word?"

Often times this question is the best place to leave the conversation. Once a policy conversation ensues, then the presenter has to be much more aware and conversant of immigration policies and the conversation can become bogged down in partisan politics or complexities of policies. Moreover, the role of presenting God's Word does not always include what the listener must do to respond. The goal of presenting the issue of immigration this way is so that God's Word can be heard by audiences that may have hardened hearts. As preachers, we send forth the Word with the faith that it will not return empty (Isa 55:11).

This style of presentation or preaching can take place in many settings and during anytime in the liturgical year. This style can be effective in preaching and especially in teaching on immigration in a discussion format with persons across the political spectrum. This lesson was most effective when I stood fast to the Bible and sought non-partisan discussions and avoided getting into the weeds on policy matters, unless I felt exceptionally equipped to do so. The remainder of this chapter will demonstrate more ways that Scripture can connect to immigration in sermons, particularly around Labor Day and then during the Advent, Christmas, and Epiphany seasons can address immigration. The chapter will conclude with exploring the power of questions to help listeners to think theologically about political issues related to immigration.

Labor-Related Sermons

Although this topic can be preached during any season of the year, the season around Labor Day is a great time to connect the topic of labor to immigration because of their deep connection in the Bible and in contemporary society. When the topic of immigrant labor was addressed in Scripture, God called for the people of Israel to protect immigrants:

> Do not take advantage of a hired man who is poor and needy, whether he is a brother Israelite or an alien living in one of your towns. Pay him his wages each day before sunset, because he is poor and is counting on it. Otherwise he may cry to the Lord against you, and you will be guilty of sin . . . Do not deprive the alien or the fatherless of justice (Deut 24:14–15, 17).

Indeed, the "Lord watches over the alien" and instructs us to do the same (Ps 146:9).

A desperate mother called me one evening and shared how her husband travelled to Corpus Christi for three weeks to hang sheetrock. At the end of those three weeks, the contractor disappeared. Because her husband had not received his salary, this mother called her pastor and shared that she was thinking about going to the *cantina* to acquire rent money. This mother of two small boys was calling her pastor to share that she was about to go prostitute herself because her husband was not paid for his labor. Her pastor worked with her to find an alternative to prostitution. However, what put her in this position was that her husband was not paid was because U.S. immigration laws prevented him from getting a work permit and made him vulnerable to abuse.

The prophet Ezekiel notes that the people of the land had fallen short of God's instruction, "The people of the land practice extortion and commit robbery; they oppress the poor and needy and mistreat the alien, denying them justice (Ezek 22:29). The people of the United States also have fallen into this same practice of mistreating foreigners as demonstrated by the treatment of the husband of the desperate mother who called me. Christians cannot faithfully treat the issue of immigration like Teflon or like children avoiding cracks in a sidewalk. The season around Labor Day is a great time for a preacher to communicate to her or his congregation the reality of laborers around them in light of Scripture and to offer congregants and listeners a way to respond to these texts through activism, organizing, and service as further examples as to how immigration can be addressed from the pulpit.

Advent, Christmas, and Epiphany Sermons

First, Christmas is the story of God immigrating to Earth. Second, Christmas is a story of hospitality, or the lack thereof. Third, out of all of the families in the history of the world and across the world into which Jesus could have been born, God chose a family that had to evade governing authorities in crossing borders. Advent, Christmas, and Epiphany are great seasons to preach on immigration, and at a minimum, these three topics can be addressed in sermons during these seasons.

First, unlike most immigrants who flee suffering seeking a better life, God left paradise and came to suffer on Earth. Why would God do that? "For God so loved the *world* that he gave his one and only Son, that whoever believes in him shall not perish but have eternal life" John 3:16 explains (*emphasis mine*). Although nations may establish political borders, God's love does not. Christ crossed borders to come to the world and demonstrated this borderless love in his encounters with persons from a variety of backgrounds. As a Palestinian Jew living under Roman occupation, Jesus noted after an encounter with a Roman centurion, "I say to you that many will come from the east and the west and will take their places at the feast with Abraham, Isaac and Jacob in the kingdom of heaven" (Matt 8:11). Jesus as the incarnation of God's love and as the model for how his followers are to love, demonstrated a borderless love.

Jesus' migration to Earth not only built a bridge between Heaven and Earth but tore down the walls that our sinful condition built to divide us and to justify discrimination, mistreatment, oppression, and injustice towards immigrants and others. Who is our neighbor and how should we express our love for them are primary questions for preachers to use in exploring immigration and border issues with their listeners in any season of the year, but especially when addressing Jesus' crossing from Heaven to Earth to give us a new law to love across borders (John 13:34–36).

Second, the Christmas story includes a story of hospitality. God's instructions to the nation of Israel and to individuals that they were to treat foreigners well continued in Christian communities through teachings on the virtue of hospitality (Tit 1:8; 1 Tim 3:2). Letters in the earliest Christian communities instructed God's people to practice hospitality (Rom 12:13; Heb 13:2; 1 Pet 4:9).

God chose Jesus' birth family with intentionality. While one can suggest reasons why and how God chose Joseph and Mary, preachers should help their listeners to explore why God choose a family that was rejected, a family that was told no room existed for them, and a family that had to leave their ancestral home to flee to a foreign land. It is doubtful that the Holy Family sought any kind of government authorization to enter into Egypt. However, Scripture makes obvious that the Holy Family did not receive permission from the government to leave Judea.

No greater revelation of God's position related to those who are forced to leave their homes and migrate exists than the Incarnation. Again, God could have chosen many families but chose a family that had to evade governing authorities. This fact is too overshadowed with pristine nativity images and ignores the political realities into which God chose to be born. In assisting congregants to see the political realities of first century Judea, preachers can help congregants navigate contemporary political realities by seeing God's consistency from the law to the incarnation of God's call to care for foreigners.

I have admired how churches have been connecting the sociopolitical reality of the Holy Family with the socio-political reality of immigrants today through marquees and through placing outdoor nativity scenes in cages similar to the cages on the U.S.–Mexico border. This messaging has been effective as it has resulted in media coverage and wide-spread social media sharing. However, a wise pastor knows that the first time a congregation connects the events of Christmas and Epiphany with the treatment of immigrants in the United States should not be on their church's marquee or in their church's nativity set. Establish the connection through teaching and preaching inside the church so that your congregants can explain your church's marquee and/or nativity scene to their friends, neighbors, and coworkers.

The Power of the Question

As all preachers know, Scripture can be connected with contemporary issues in many ways. Immigration is no different. *Lifting up questions* without blatantly answering the questions can assist listeners into thinking theologically about issues without listeners feeling like their preacher is telling them what to think or like the preacher is forcing their political opinions upon them.

In the section "Standing Fast to Scripture," I presented the strategy of sharing various texts related to immigration in Scripture and then asking the question, "If the United States of America were a Christian nation, not a democracy as we are, but a Christian theocracy with our laws based primarily if not exclusively on the Bible, what would our immigration policy look like?" Again, this question would be followed with the question, "Now we understand what God's Word says about immigrants and immigration, how shall we respond to God's word in our behaviors, attitudes, and voting?" The presenter does not need to answer the questions for this to be an effective means of assisting persons to think theologically about immigration.

Some examples of questions during Advent, Christmas, and Epiphany seasons that can help listeners to think theologically about the Incarnation and what it means for how believers respond to families born into similar circumstances as our Lord's include:

- Why did God choose a poor family rather than a rich family?

- Why did God choose a family that would have to travel by government mandate for a census while his mom was well into her pregnancy with him?

- Why did God choose a family that had to evade governing authorities while crossing borders?

- If God was to be born today in similar circumstances as Jesus was born, what would those circumstances be?

- If the Incarnation happened in the Western Hemisphere, today where would we find the social circumstances most like the social circumstances of Jesus' birth 2000 years ago?

- The Magi helped a refugee family who sought asylum in Egypt. If Egypt had similar laws as the U.S. has today, what could you do as an individual, as a family, as a congregation, and as a voter and citizen of the United States, to respond to help families similar to our Lord's family today?

Again, the questions do not need to be answered in order to have their effect. At times, answering the questions is the right technique. At other times, the preacher can simply leave the listeners to ponder the questions.

Conclusion

A simple search of the news about how asylum seekers are being treated at the U.S. border, about how immigrants are being treated in prisons, about how immigrant communities are being terrorized by raids, and about multiple other means foreigners are being mistreated by the U.S. government and by nativist and abusive employers in the U.S. will provide ample content for any preacher to address immigration issues in light of the Scriptures shared in this chapter. Left without the guidance of preachers, many congregants are left to cable news pundits to guide them how to think about political issues.

I was wrong for ever treating immigration like Teflon. I had not been exposed to these texts relating to immigration or had never made the connection between some texts that obviously deal with immigration. I was blinded to the obvious way Scripture addresses immigration.

My experience in living and working in the Christ's Foundry immigrant community exposed me to first-hand knowledge of how the U.S.'s abandonment of Christian values around immigration enforcement was inflicting horrific suffering on immigrant families. As a preacher who was silent on this issue, I was unfaithful. God was calling me to audaciously and unabashedly speak out on issues of immigration that were affecting the Christ's Foundry community and beyond. Scripture not only commanded that I no longer treat the issue of immigration like Teflon, Scripture *convicted me* and *equipped me* to be able to address issues of immigration in diverse settings as well as in distinctly conservative settings where audiences held opinions on immigration that were contrary to mine.

Matthew 6:33 teaches that when we seek the Kingdom of God and God's justice first, everything else will be added. Seeking God's Kingdom and God's justice today includes addressing how the United States is mistreating immigrants and asylum seekers. Immigration policies and their enforcement are only getting worse. Anti-immigrant sentiments are growing, and Christians are complicit. Some preachers are misleading listeners in addressing issues of immigration while other pastors avoid texts related to immigration like my kids hopping around cracks in old sidewalks. Other preachers bring partisan politics so much into their teachings that they appear co-opted by a political party and do not present the gospel in ways that persons of other political parties can hear.

However, more and more courageous preachers like the ones reading this book are seeking to be faithful, are seeking God's Kingdom, and are seeking God's justice. The Church, the United States, and indeed, the world needs more prophetic voices like those reading this book. To clarify, prophecy is not about reading the future; prophecy is about reading the present. What is going on in our world and what does God want your listeners to know about it? What is God doing and how is God inviting your listeners to participate in God's activity? If preachers in the United States do not speak up in the tradition of the prophets to prick our collective conscience, who will? When it comes to preaching on issues of immigration, Scripture is our richest resource. Proclaim it, preacher!

9

Toward a Border-Crossing Homiletic

Building Blocks for Trauma-Informed Preaching Practices

—LIS VALLE

S ome of the most vulnerable people near the USA/Mexico border are
those who risk their lives in the desert and are raped in the process of
crossing the border. Many churches respond with water, food, shelter, and
sanctuary, activities that happen outside corporate worship and preaching.
Although not all preachers are also professional mental health care providers, they may still engage in trauma-informed preaching and thus collaborate
in the recovery process. This essay draws on American psychiatrist Judith
L. Herman's theoretical framework of recovery for healing from trauma, to
propose a border-crossing homiletic that is trauma-informed.

Trauma-informed practices may help churches avoid the mistakes of
Tamar's family. In 2 Sam 13:14–19, Tamar, daughter of King David, does
her best to persuade with words her brother Amnon not to rape her. Tamar
explicitly requested, "do not force me . . . do not do anything so vile!" She
made an ethical claim. She reminded him of what behavior was deemed
contemptible in Israel and what the consequences would be for both of
them. When he ordered her to leave, she even proposed an alternative so he
could have her without dishonoring their household. Nonetheless, Amnon
did not listen to her, neither before nor after. He twice ignored her words
and so she resorted to actions to communicate her grievance as she went
to her brother Absalom. He offered her sanctuary, but in the process he

also silenced her, warning and cajoling her, "Be quiet for now, my sister; he is your brother; do not take this to heart." Thus, her rapist Amnon ignored Tamar's voice, and her protector Absalom shushed her. Two years later Absalom did indeed avenge the violation of his sister, but she had no opportunity to recover her power or social connections. She "remained, a desolate woman, in her brother Absalom's house."

What?

Similar to Tamar, today the most vulnerable of border crossers are being violated and shushed. About sixty[1] to eighty percent[2] of Latin American women crossing the US/Mexico border are raped during their journey.[3] The lived experience of these women is what grounds this proposal for border-crossing preaching. The aftermath of the violence that survivors have suffered affects preaching and biblical interpretation by challenging preachers to become homiletical border crossers. Homiletical border-crossing facilitates recovery through the creation of conditions during the preaching moment that increase the safety, agency, remembrance, mourning, and social connections of parishioners. In light of the physical assault that people suffer, some preachers do already tackle biblical texts with similar stories in special healing services (a ministry that is best implemented bearing in mind particular considerations that are beyond the scope of this essay).

Preachers are not necessarily experts in diagnosing, or treating people with trauma, nor is the pulpit the place for such services. Nonetheless, border-crossing preachers can indeed develop trauma-informed sermons by getting acquainted with trauma theory and its goals, and by developing preaching practices informed by such theory. Furthermore, while not all immigrants have suffered sexualized violence or trauma, all immigrants have experienced in their bodies the crossing of borders. In addition, the goals of empowerment and social connections are good goals for any human being, not only immigrants, and are goals consonant with values of the gospel, such as love of neighbor, human dignity based on *imago dei*, divine justice and desire for liberation from evil and oppression. Thus, trauma-informed sermons are likely to be life-giving to all humans who witness them and can also be appropriate for any given worship service and any given biblical text.

1. Amnesty International.
2. McIntyre and Bonello, "Is Rape the Price?"
3. Fernández, "You Have to Pay with Your Body."

Trauma, Recovery, and Preaching

Trauma-informed preaching is a task for border-crossing people who facilitate collective biblical interpretation in the midst of the congregation. This essay establishes correlations between homiletic theory and Judith L. Herman's theoretical framework of recovery for healing from trauma. Specifically, the focus is on the two goals of recovery (empowerment and social connections), and the three stages of recovery (safety; reconstruction of story; and reconnection). These correlations lead to a trauma-informed preaching practice with a distinctive approach to the preacher's role, hermeneutics for preaching, and delivery of sermons.

Herman's framework is based on well-documented research and about two decades of clinical work. Drawing on the experiences of survivors of sexual and domestic abuse, the Holocaust, and war, Herman observes that traumatic syndromes have two common features: disempowerment of the survivor and disconnection from others. Consequently, she concludes that the goals of recovery are empowerment of the survivor and the creation of new social connections. Upon these basic principles, Herman develops a conceptual framework for psychotherapy with traumatized people consisting of three fundamental stages of recovery: establishing safety, reconstructing the trauma story, and restoring the connection between survivors and their community. Each stage has a corresponding central task: establishment of safety; remembrance and mourning; and reconnection with ordinary life. The interelation of the three non-linear stages of recovery and the two basic principles of empowerment and reconnection allows for the development of a border crossing homiletic characterized by trauma-informed preaching practices.

Empowerment and Social Connections

The goals of trauma-informed preaching are empowerment and social connection. When preachers align the preaching task to these goals, they might cross borders in ways that facilitate recovery. Preachers are border-crossing people because preaching happens in the borderlands, at the border between human and divine natures. The pulpit is a place where the divine Word is proclaimed through human speech, as Charles Bartow has affirmed.[4] When preaching is also mindful of the situations that af-

4 Bartow, *God's Human Speech.*

fect life in the geographical borders of the land, and seeks to produce trauma-informed sermons, then preachers are challenged to take greater risks in crossing borders in the pulpit. Preachers may cross additional borders by defying expectations, by increasing the agency and roles of the listeners, and by sharing power, authority, and voice at the pulpit. As a result, border-crossing preachers will facilitate a certain kind of collective biblical interpretation in the midst of the community to nurture empowerment and social connections.

In search of preaching practices that advance the empowerment of parishioners and nurture their social connections, I propose this correlation between Herman's stages of recovery and trauma-informed preaching practices. I correlate the stage of safety with the role of the preacher; suggest that reconstruction of story relates to communal biblical interpretation; and that reconnection with community is the basis for collective delivery of the sermon. The role of the preacher understood as both host and guest through the sermon provides hospitality and sanctuary to survivors of systemic oppression, a safer space for them to speak their truth. Methods of situated hermeneutics and theories of testimonial preaching provide liturgical structure for empowering worshipers through collective biblical interpretation in light of their lived experience, thus reconstructing stories. Theories on healing and conversational preaching allow for the creation of new social connections.

Safety and the Role of the Preacher

In a border-crossing homiletic the preacher takes the risk of being a facilitator of a conversation instead of a lecturer. The preacher's role becomes that of host and guest as a way of restoring power and control to survivors over body and environment, securing a safe refuge, and widening the sphere of authority of survivors. If the preaching moment will widen the sphere of authority of worshipers, preachers need to share their authority with those who are otherwise listeners.

One of the many ways in which a preacher may restore to worshipers their power over body and environment, widening the sphere of their authority, is by acting as a host during the preparation for the preaching moment. In comparing the role of the preacher to that of a host, John Mc-Clure explains in his essay "Preacher as Host and Guest," that the preacher as host has the responsibility to protect the welcoming space and the rights of the guests in relation to that space. This involves ascertaining the identity of the strangers being welcomed, discerning their intentions, and protecting the safety and voices of the guests.[5] By doing these three tasks, the preacher as host holds space for people to engage in dialogue and nurtures a sense of sanctuary. Preachers may perform these tasks by establishing a prior relationship of trust with parishioners, having either a general idea of their theological stances or more particularly of their interpretation of a specific biblical text prior to sharing the pulpit with them, and respecting their interpretations even when they differ from the preacher's interpretation. These are some ways in which preachers may serve as hosts in order to secure a safe refuge in which parishioners can speak their truth.

After securing this safe refuge, border-crossing preachers then invite survivors to exercise control over the process of reading their life story through scripture, and reading scripture through their life story—as opposed to doing it for them, which would only perpetuate their lack of agency. A preacher may do this by hosting a collaborative working relationship characterized by mutuality through fluidity of roles in border-crossing preaching. Here McClure is once again helpful. In explaining the roles of host and guest, he builds on the ancient practice of hospitality in the Christian tradition to offer the image of an itinerant preacher (Jesus and Paul serving as examples) who is by necessity hosted but becomes a host by leading a conversation in which the preacher together with the guests collaboratively discern a new truth. McClure encourages preachers to be hosts by welcoming strangers into the preaching ministry, and to be guests when those strangers suggest new possibilities for interpreting the biblical text.[6] Survivors' sphere of authority widens when they are included in the process of sermon preparation and delivery—or any power-sharing activity. They are guests of the preacher in the preparation and delivery of the sermon, and they host the preacher through offering their personal stories and particular interpretations. When the preacher acts as host and guest, the parishioners, who are acting as co-preachers, are also participating as hosts and guests in a relation of mutuality, and they are able to exercise their agency by being in control of their bodies and their environment. Their inclusion in the process contributes to the first stage of recovery—that of establishing safety through restoring power over body and environment and widening the sphere of their authority.

5. McClure, "Preacher as Host and Guest," 132–34.
6. McClure, "Preacher as Host and Guest," 119–23.

Reconstructing the Story and Communal Hermeneutics

In a border-crossing homiletic the preacher takes the risk of facilitating a process of communal biblical interpretation. As the congregation serves as the audience or witnessing community, some of the members reconstruct stories in community, thus serving as co-preachers. Herman's trauma theory along with methods of situated hermeneutics and theories of testimonial preaching together show how preaching may facilitate reconstruction of stories. Herman's second stage of recovery, reconstructing the trauma story, may be evident in a sermon if the co-preachers tell their personal stories and give witness to what they perceive in scripture from the perspective of their lived experience.

Herman establishes that the main tasks of the second stage of recovery are remembrance and mourning so that survivors may experience a gradual shift from dissociated trauma to acknowledged memory. During this stage, survivors recount the traumatic event, reconstruct the memory, thus effectively transforming it, and mourn their losses. During this stage, the need to empower the survivor and to preserve their safety remains. This process involves a systematic review of the meaning of the event. Throughout, the role of the therapist is to stay neutral and nonjudgmental, affirm a position of moral solidarity with survivors, and to faithfully bear witness to their story as ally and witness. Relying on the restorative power of truth-telling, and given that psychotherapy cannot get rid of the trauma completely, the goal of telling the story is integration so that the person "reclaims her own history and feels renewed hope and energy for engagement with life."[7] Through recounting the traumatic event, transforming the memory, and mourning the losses, survivors continue to achieve the goal of integration.

Recounting the story, transforming the memory, and mourning the loss have an intrinsic relationship. They are aspects of reconstructing the trauma story that are hard to keep separate. Border-crossing preachers need to consider these three aspects in order to be effective. Drawing on methods of situated hermeneutics border-crossing preachers may prepare to facilitate and participate in communal hermeneutics. Furthermore, drawing on theories of testimony, the concepts of counter-testimony and lament may serve as homiletical strategies to facilitate the remembrance and mourning that survivors need in the second stage of recovery identified by Herman. Through the combination of these forms of biblical interpretation,

7. Herman, *Trauma and Recovery*, 195.

border-crossing preachers facilitate communal hermeneutics to help co-preachers and listeners reconstruct their life stories in light of scripture, and scripture stories in light of their lived experiences.

Situated hermeneutics, such as the Hispanic hermeneutical model and mujerista biblical interpretation, are useful tools for border-crossing preachers. In *Púlpito: An Introduction to Hispanic Preaching*, Pablo A. Jiménez, and Justo L. González explain how the Hispanic hermeneutical model works. Their approach offers a reading of resistance to the Bible as liberating text focusing on the eschatological dimension of the text and nurturing hope born out of a hurtful past. The method includes marginality as entry point to the text, which in the case under discussion would be the marginality of immigrants and life in the borderlands. Jiménez and González summarize the method stating, "It is clear that the true key to this hermeneutical model is the correlation between the social location of the Bible and the social location of the Latino people. However, this model can be very useful for non-Hispanic preachers who want to engage the Bible in a new way."[8] Likewise, mujerista biblical interpretation invites preachers to put the experience of Latin American women at the center when interpreting sacred texts. In her essay, "La Palabra de Dios en Nosotras" (The Word of God in Us), Ada María Isasi Díaz states that mujerista biblical interpretation uses the lived experience of Latina women as the starting point, utilizing scripture when and as needed to advance the goal of communal liberation-salvation.[9] The Hispanic hermeneutical model and mujerista biblical interpretation disrupt the way that preachers perceive and interpret the text, in turn generating interpretations that disrupt the text and the life of the listeners for the sake of liberation.

Situated hermeneutics may include perceiving the text through the standpoint of many other different life experiences. For example, in *The Witness of Preaching*, Thomas G. Long encourages preachers to listen attentively to the text, to question, and interrogate it. One of the strategies that Long offers to question the text is to view the text through many different "eyes." Long offers many examples. Adapting Long's examples for the purposes of preaching that considers the borderlands, the preacher may add to Long's list questions such as, "How would this passage appear to . . . immigrants? . . . border crossers? . . . survivors of rape? The preacher may arrange for exegesis to take place prior to the worship service in a group setting and

8. Jiménez and González, *Púlpito*, 46.

9. Isasi-Díaz, *Mujerista Theology*, 148–69.

actually hear the reactions of a variety of people. John McClure offers a comprehensive method on how to accomplish such a task in his book *The Roundtable Pulpit*.[10] When a system for communal exegesis is not in place, the preacher may imagine the presence of a diverse group, as Long suggests, or may have one-on-one conversations with a variety of people, asking them what they perceive in the text. The product of such conversations will prepare the preacher to better contextualize the product of the exegesis and the interpretation of the text, as well as to facilitate communal biblical interpretation in the midst of the congregation. Preachers who rely only on their own imaginations, Long warns, "cannot, and should not, presume to know how all these people would respond and must therefore always be reading, studying, and listening to the voices of people unlike themselves."[11] Different eyes deepen exegesis because they notice distinctive dimensions of the text beyond literary and sociohistorical criticism.

In a border-crossing homiletic the preacher takes the risk of facilitating a process of communal biblical interpretation. Herman's trauma theory along with methods of situated hermeneutics, and theories of testimonial preaching together show how preaching may facilitate reconstruction of stories. Furthermore, Herman's second stage of recovery, reconstructing the trauma story, may be evident in a sermon if the co-preachers tell their personal stories and give witness to what they perceive in scripture in light of their lived experience.

In addition to situated hermeneutics, notions of complaint or lament aid in the task of reconstructing stories through communal biblical interpretation. Lament allows the telling of personal stories with the purpose of summoning God back to power and solidarity. Through liturgies of lament worshipers are able to recount and transform fragmented memories and ascribe new meanings to them. Brueggemann calls this process "Cadences that Redescribe." He resorts to lamentation and complaint as liturgical genres that allow exiles, or in this case, survivors, to move from the shattering of their paradigms of meaning toward newly voiced meaning; or away from conventional descriptions and explanations toward re-describing reality.[12] In this kind of lament, "it is the one who experiences the dismay who must courageously come to speech."[13] Testimonial

10. McClure, *Roundtable Pulpit*.

11. Long, *Witness of Preaching*, 86–87.

12 Brueggemann, *Cadences of Home*, 15.

13 Brueggemann, *Cadences of Home*, 18.

preaching in the form of lament told by the survivor includes the personal story, but most importantly it constitutes a re-construction that allows for the transformation of memory that is necessary for recovery while also generating fresh theological insights.

This re-construction of stories happens before a faith community in worship that serves as an audience. This is consonant with Israel's practices of witness and testimony. One of these practices that Brueggemann identifies in his essay "Testimony as a Decentered Mode of Preaching" responds to a liturgical formula. He explains, "The liturgy invites Israel to witness to **evidence from its own life**, and thereby to **construct an alternative account** of reality in which Yahweh is credible, normal, and indispensable."[14] The primary audience of this mode of testimony is the people in the liturgy, but the testimony is also intended to address those outside the community. Co-preachers can testify in the midst of liturgy, and the people gathered would be the witnessing audience.

Furthermore, the people in the liturgy will serve as "communities of honest sadness" that join survivors in naming and mourning the losses.[15] The community of honest sadness not only names and mourns the losses, but should do so in a nonjudgmental spirit in order to provide the safe space that survivors need. In this sense, the community shows compassion without blaming the victim, suffering with them but also hoping for better and pushing toward a new quality of life.[16] Furthermore, a community of honest sadness facilitates grief by loaning "each other the strength and support we sometimes cannot muster from our own reserves."[17] For this mourning to occur, Brueggemann suggests a structure based on his analysis of the book of Lamentations which begins with negativity produced by the traumatic event, ends in questioning God for abandoning them, and expresses negotiation between sadness and hope.[18] The dynamics and structure of communities of honest sadness facilitate in liturgy the tasks of the second stage of recovery: those of remembrance and mourning by witnessing to survivors' suffering and joining them in mourning the losses.

---

14. Brueggemann, *Cadences of Home*, 49 (emphasis added).

15. Brueggemann, *Cadences of Home*, 4.

16. Shoop, *Let the Bones Dance*, 132–33.

17. Nichols, *Restoring Word*, 41.

18. Brueggemann, *Cadences of Home*, 4–5.

Social Connections and Collective Delivery

In a border-crossing homiletic, the preacher facilitates collective delivery of the sermon. Border-crossing preachers take the risk of performing the process of communal interpretation before the worshiping community. Herman's third stage of recovery, restoring the connection between survivors and their community, may be accomplished during a sermon in which the co-preachers connect with each other and with the community through communal biblical interpretation performed through conversational preaching.

Herman establishes that the main task of the third stage of recovery is reconnection with ordinary life so that survivors experience a gradual shift from stigmatized isolation to restored social connections. During this stage, the core experiences of helplessness and isolation need to be countered with empowerment, reconnection, and new relationships. Through re-creating the self and reconnecting with others, survivors are able to reconnect with ordinary life in this third stage of recovery, moving from isolation to restored social connections.

Preaching may help this process of restoring connections in many ways. Through appropriate use of biblical imagery to balance individual autonomy and close social relationships, emphasis on healing as opposed to cure,[19] and invitations to cross religious and cultural boundaries for the sake of connecting with excluded people, preaching may facilitate the third stage of recovery for survivors. In addition, border-crossing preachers may draw on conversational preaching to further facilitate the tasks of the third stage of recovery.

Lucy Atkins Rose's conversational preaching offers a way for preaching to facilitate immigrants' movement out of isolation and into the faith community. The aim of conversational preaching is to "gather the community of faith around the Word where the central conversations of the people of God are fostered and refocused week after week."[20] This aim in itself seeks the restoration of connections between preacher and congregation. It is the preacher who Rose identifies as isolated and she argues for bridging the gap between preacher and congregation by putting into action the priesthood of all believers. According to Rose, the result is an experience of connectedness. Additionally, Rose states that one of the characteristics at the heart

19. Black, *A Healing Homiletic.*
20. Rose, *Sharing the Word,* 93.

of conversational preaching is that it is communal. In explaining the communal aspect of preaching, Rose compares the gathered community with a family or a household that nurtures a larger sense of connectedness by discerning the Word together. Following theologian Letty M. Russell, Rose explains that Christ is the host of the household while simultaneously located on the periphery of church and society with the outsiders. The implication is that conversational preaching by necessity nurtures the connectedness of the community of faith both internally and externally. By bridging the gap between preacher and congregation and between "insiders" and "outsiders," conversational preaching offers a way of facilitating the reconnection that survivors need during the third stage of the recovery process.

It was not Rose's intention for conversational sermons to be dialogue sermons or interactive sermons, though she admitted that these forms might lend themselves to conversational preaching. However, dialogue or interactive sermons may bridge the gap between preacher and congregation and bring co-preachers in. During the worship service, co-preachers may be physically located around the Word to discern it, while the rest of the faith community gathers around them witnessing. The proclamation may literally be a conversation among the preachers with scripture. This approach to preaching moves those who would otherwise be listeners from isolation to connectedness through conversational preaching.

In conclusion, Rose's conversational preaching offers ways to understand how preaching can restore social connections for survivors of sexual abuse or nurture social connections for marginalized border crossers. Preachers may use this conceptual framework to facilitate the third stage of recovery from trauma, restoration of social connections. Preachers may bridge the gap between themselves and the congregation and between the church and the ostracized by resorting to conversational preaching in order to restore connections between co-preachers and their communities.

Conclusion

Tamar's family tried their best after Amnon didn't listen to Tamar's voice and raped her. King David got angry. Absalom provided sanctuary, silenced Tamar, and avenged her. Today, thanks to trauma theory, preachers know that Tamar also needed empowerment and reconnection in order to recover. Border-crossing preachers may draw on the Jewish and Christian traditions and modern homiletic theories to make preaching a safer space in which border crossers can reconstruct their stories in conversation with Scripture and with their faith community as co-interpreter and witness. Border-crossing preachers take risks to offer a safe haven in the preaching moment in order that the people of God be empowered and re-connected. Against the violence that dehumanizes all kinds of border crossers, preaching offers them a space to live into their full humanity. Border-crossing preachers and service providers, like Absalom, offer sanctuary to the most vulnerable. However, border-crossing preachers would notice that Absalom silenced Tamar as much as Amnon did, and that David—king and father—ignored Tamar's voice. Therefore, border-crossing preachers and community leaders, unlike Amnon, Absalom, and David, would listen to the voices of the most vulnerable, let them speak for themselves, and respect their agency so that persons living in the borderlands do not remain desolate people in the house of their siblings. Así nos ayude Dios.

10

Comrades of the Kin-dom[1]

Mark 6:14–29

—REBECCA DAVID HENSLEY

Background

This sermon was delivered on July 15, 2018, at Grace United Methodist Church in Dallas, Texas, where I served as Associate Pastor at the time. Serving the Downtown/East Dallas area for over 115 years, Grace UMC is progressive in its theology and traditional in its worship experience. Throughout the week, its ministries include: a preschool, a medical clinic, a legal clinic, a sanctuary for teen mothers, a new monastic community serving the poor, and a community center. The membership of Grace UMC is primarily white and middle-class, with a "vibrant mix of people from different backgrounds, ethnicities, cultures, sexualities, and genders as well as people with disabilities."[2]

The primary scripture for this sermon is Mark 6:14–29, the Revised Common Lectionary gospel text for the day, supplemented by Luke 4:16–30.

---

1. The term "kin-dom" comes from the work of *mujerista* theologian Ada María Isasi-Díaz, who used the term as a way of expressing the familial bonds within the body of Christ, while countering the patriarchal structures inherent within the concept of "kingdom."

2. Grace United Methodist Church, Dallas, "Welcome to Grace Church." www.graceumcdallas.org.

At the time this sermon was preached, protests and prophetic actions were occurring throughout the nation, as millions were outraged at the "Zero Tolerance" policies of the Trump administration which forced the separation of families and detention of children and minors along the U.S./Mexico border. In border states like Texas, this political circus and human tragedy was playing out in our own backyard. Having personally witnessed the faces of precious little ones, from toddlers to children no more than ten years old, peering through the bars of a prison bus transporting them from the Ursula Processing Center in McAllen, Texas to an undisclosed location, this sermon was my faithful response to the cruelty of our nation's border control policies enacted at this time. Furthermore, as a White citizen of a country deeply dependent upon the labor of our immigrants, born and with longstanding family farming roots in Harlingen, Texas (approximately twenty miles north of the Mexico border), I preach this sermon as part of my faithful response to my own privilege in a culture that simultaneously beckons and denies the biblical mandate to welcome the foreigner.

My prayer for you, dear reader, is that it will encourage you to preach boldly and prophetically, even when (*especially* when) the stakes are high— whether you choose your scripture from week to week, create your own topical series, or preach directly from the lectionary. As our nation continues to struggle with its own humanity at the U.S./Mexico border—including the deaths of seven-year-old Jakelin Amei Rosmery Caal Maquin and eight-year-old Felipe Gómez Alonzo while in the custody of U.S. Border Patrol in El Paso, Texas—your prophetic resistance is a necessary form of revolutionary love. Indeed, *it is* the gospel itself for our times.

Sermon Text

If you noticed the sermon title for this morning, coupled with the scripture about the beheading of John the Baptist, and thought to yourself, "Is she planning to convert us all to some militant form of communism?"—you can rest easy. That is not my goal. What I want to focus on today is what it really means to be a comrade for the kin-dom of God. It might be helpful, then, to give a brief definition of what I mean by "comrade." In a secular sense, there is a difference between a comrade and a friend. As the saying goes, a friend is someone you can count on to bail you out of jail. But a comrade is someone who will be sitting in jail *with* you!

From a spiritual perspective, we might interpret the term "comrade" as a way of expressing what it means to be in true *communion* with a God who loved the world enough to take on our flesh, and in so doing, commit his very life to the cause of freedom, dignity, and the reconciliation of all humanity with God and one another. Jesus was extremely clear on this. And lest you think I was just digging around for some brutal biblical encounter to preach on this my final Sunday with you all, I assure you, this week's text comes straight out of the lectionary and it immediately follows the gospel text from last week. The author of Mark sandwiches this account of John, Jesus' mentor—his comrade—in between Jesus' commissioning of the disciples and their return. Why would he do that? This is an *awful* story—and an even worse recruitment tool! Who wants to be commissioned into a movement that might literally cost you your head?!?

Here's where I find it helpful to invoke a little literary criticism of the gospel of Mark. Generally speaking, Mark is a great book for those who like to skim the details, hit the highlights, and then quickly move on to the next thing. It's often referred to as "the gospel of immediacy" because nearly everything in it happens *immediately*. In fact, the word "immediately" appears something like forty times throughout its sixteen short chapters. But the problem with Mark's gospel, in my opinion, is that the author is in such a hurry, the audience misses out on some important texture and detail along the way.

For instance, in Mark's account of Jesus' rejection at Nazareth, he fails to mention what in the world Jesus said or did to offend the people so badly. This is where I think Luke's audience gets much more bang for their gospel-reading buck! While we can't assume these two gospel writers had the same intentions for their respective audiences—we can look to Luke's account as one possibility that adds a little more texture to Jesus' rejection at his hometown. I invite you to grab your Bible and turn to Luke 4, beginning with verse sixteen:

> When he came to Nazareth, where he had been brought up, he went to the synagogue on the sabbath day, as was his custom. He stood up to read, and the scroll of the prophet Isaiah was given to him. He unrolled the scroll and found the place where it was written:
>
> 'The Spirit of the Lord is upon me,
>
>   because he has anointed me

> to bring good news to the poor.

> He has sent me to proclaim release to the captives

> and recovery of sight to the blind,

> to let the oppressed go free,

> to proclaim the year of the Lord's favour.'

> And he rolled up the scroll, gave it back to the attendant, and sat down. The eyes of all in the synagogue were fixed on him. Then he began to say to them, 'Today this scripture has been fulfilled in your hearing.'[3]

Now at first, Luke's gospel tells us the people were *amazed*—as in, they were feeling rather proud of their hometown boy! But then, he said something that caused them to turn; something that caused them to get so angry they tried to run him off a cliff! *What did he say?*

Basically, he began speaking prophetically. He spoke truth to power— truth to his hometown—and they didn't like it. He referenced the work of Elijah and Elisha: the prophets who welcomed, fed, cared for, and healed outsiders from foreign lands. Luke 4:28 says, "When they heard this, all in the synagogue were filled with rage." With *rage*! Sound familiar? Do you know anyone who is filled with rage these days when it comes to welcoming people from foreign lands—the migrant worker, the border crosser, the refugee? Do any of the ones filled with rage come from your hometown? From your own family, perhaps?

Jesus was clear throughout his ministry, regardless of which gospel we read: there is no room in his mission for hatred and exclusion of any of God's children. There is no room for building borders between those we choose to love, and those we choose to cast aside. There is no room for abandoning or mistreating mothers seeking safety and provision for their children. There is no room for refusing refugees who are seeking asylum and healing from the horrific violence that threatens their lives every day.

As we witness the current events unfolding at our nation's border—at our *state's* border—we are also witnessing a growing number of prophetic voices rising up to proclaim the gospel truth that if you are a disciple of Jesus, there is no "zero tolerance" for immigrants. There is no "zero tolerance" for asylum seekers. There is no "zero tolerance" for parents who've made a treacherous journey on a hope and a prayer that their children might have

---

3 Luke 4:16–21. New Revised Standard Version [all scripture references in this chapter are NRSV].

a safer existence. There is no "zero tolerance" for toddlers, grade school children, and teens—many of whom have made that treacherous journey *without their parents*—trying to reach that same dream of freedom to simply make it to adulthood without being murdered or forced to join gangs and become murderers themselves.

No, Jesus doesn't have a "zero tolerance" policy for the children and families attempting to cross our man-made border. Instead, Jesus has a few "zero tolerance" policies of his own:

- "Zero tolerance" for racism; for sexism; for xenophobia.
- "Zero tolerance" for white supremacy.
- "Zero tolerance" for the for-profit prison industrial complex that has led to mass incarceration in jails and detention centers, leaving both immigrant *and citizen* families ripped apart.
- "Zero tolerance" for systemic greed that benefits from the gifts and the labor of migrant workers, but then degrades and strips them of their humanity.
- "Zero tolerance" for treating *any* of God's children as unworthy of the love of God and the dignity of a life lived to the fullest.

Given *this* was the mission Jesus was trying to fulfill—and knowing the current events unfolding in our nation, and the polarization many of us feel between ourselves and our fellow citizens, coworkers, friends, and even family members—perhaps it makes a little more sense that Mark's gospel follows the rejection of Jesus with this account of John's beheading. It's essentially Mark's way of saying, "It's hard out here for a prophet." Many scholars believe this reference to John the Baptist is a Good Friday story—a reminder of the dark before the dawn; a foreshadowing of the events that will unfold for Jesus later in the gospel. But it's also a fore*warning*: If you choose to be disciples of Jesus, there will be sacrifice involved. It might even cost you your life.

I spent a week in El Salvador last March with a group from Perkins School of Theology. Of the many profound and unforgettable experiences shared on that trip, the most holy and soul-stirring moment was our visit to the chapel where Archbishop Oscar Romero was assassinated. When Romero was first appointed as the Catholic Archbishop of San Salvador in 1977, he didn't plan to become the great father of the country's liberation movement. In fact, those who appointed him thought he would be helpful in keeping the masses in check. But as he began to hear the stories of the people—*el pueblo*—his heart was moved to preach "good news to the poor"—to *these* poor; the ones right there in his very real and immediate context; his own people who were extremely oppressed by a government that sought to wipe out most of the peasantry and essentially enslave those who remained. He consistently preached a theology of liberation to el pueblo and a message of agape love to the government and military officials, beseeching them to see their fellow countrymen as their brothers and sisters. Serving only three years in his role as Archbishop, he was assassinated while celebrating Mass in a small chapel at Hospital de la Divina Providencia, the place he chose to reside so he could be close to the suffering of the patients there. And while I have read and revered Romero as a prophetic spiritual leader for many years, it was in that little chapel where I felt I truly "met him" for the first time. . .

My classmates and I solemnly approached the altar where Romero preached his last sermon and prepared to give el pueblo the bread of life and the cup of salvation. We prayed and we cried as we stood in the very space where his body had once lain, bleeding and dying—literally giving his life to the cause of liberation. It was heavy. It was somber. It was a holy moment. And it was also a stark reminder of the (sometimes fatal) cost of discipleship. Romero's assassins knew the power of the moment they chose to complete their mission. They knew the power of el pueblo resided in the power of community—*la comunidad*. And they knew there was no moment more impactful for them to attempt to stamp out that power, than the very moment when la communidad gathered together to celebrate Holy Communion.

"Resucitaré en el pueblo salvadoreño"—I will rise again in the Salvadoran people. Romero spoke these fateful words just weeks before he was killed. Like so many martyrs before him—Martin Luther King, Bonhoeffer, Jesus—it was as if Romero knew his time had drawn short, and the only thing he could do was embrace every moment of this life, working for the kin-dom of God to come upon the earth. And to this day, his spirit continues to rise in el pueblo—not only in El Salvador, but throughout the entire world. Later this year, he will be canonized as a Saint in the Catholic Church. But he didn't become a saint, or even the spiritual leader of a nation, without first becoming a comrade of the people. And for his people, he gave his life.

Friends, I don't know what it will cost us to become true comrades with the families who are suffering at our nation's border. But I do know that Jesus' mission was clear and unwavering, even unto his death. I know that John the Baptist served as a mentor to him—and when the stakes were high, John didn't shy away from speaking truth to power. He had no idea what the consequences would be when he called out the highest government official for his deeds of misconduct. (Marital misconduct, for that matter, but we'll save that for another sermon!) But John spoke the truth anyway. He had to know that Herod was surrounded by family members and other authority figures who were malicious, conniving, and vindictive—after all, he was arrested, bound, and thrown in prison by Herod's men. But he couldn't possibly have known how such seemingly unbelievable events would unfold like a scene straight out of Game of Thrones! And yet, he spoke the truth anyway.

Often in social justice movements, people speak of "putting your body on the line" for the cause. And often they are dismissed, perhaps by people from hometowns like Nazareth, who claim they're just radicals who are breaking the law and deserve whatever consequences they provoke. But where do we think "putting your body on the line" comes from? John the Baptist didn't have to call out Herod's misconduct. He could have kept silent for the sake of a false civility or to please the crowd. But he spoke truth to power. And Jesus followed his mentor in doing the same thing. He could've backed down when the authorities questioned him. Instead, he stood firm in who he was—and he went to the cross for it.

Countless men, women, and children led the Civil Rights Movement of the 1950s–1960s by putting their bodies on the line. Sit-ins, boycotts, Bloody Sunday, Freedom Summer—all of it involved real life *bodies*, people who withstood beatings, imprisonment, and even death—to resist evil, injustice, and oppression in whatever forms they present themselves. . . just like our baptismal vows bid us to do.[4]

And as we can see, their work is not yet complete. *We* are the ones who are now charged with carrying forward the cause of freedom and dignity for all. I do not know what sacrifices each of us need to make as we pick up the mantle of the prophetic witnesses that have gone before us. Perhaps it is simply the sacrifice of a few moments of our time to contact

---

4. The Baptismal Covenant vows taken by persons (or on behalf of persons unable to answer for themselves) being baptized in the United Methodist Church. *The United Methodist Hymnal,* 33–43.

our elected officials. Perhaps it will cost us some tension at the next holiday gathering as we speak truth to our family members who don't want to hear about a God who welcomes immigrants and refugees. Perhaps it will cost us relationships with family, friends, or coworkers who simply refuse to see the image of God in the faces of children encaged at our nation's border. Perhaps it will cost some of us arrest and imprisonment as we refuse to abide by unjust laws that demean human dignity. Perhaps it will cost this church body the time and dedication it takes to become a sanctuary or solidarity congregation.

I do not know what the sacrifice will be for you—or for me. But this is what I do know: there are still over 2,000 children awaiting reunification with their families, and conflicting reports over whether more children continue to be separated. These children have already put their bodies on the line to come to this country. They have endured far more than most of us could ever imagine on their journey to this point. And every day they continue to sit imprisoned in a concentration camp for kids, built and maintained by our government—*financed by us*—is another day that mental, emotional, and spiritual harm is being inflicted upon them. There is no "zero tolerance" policy for immigrants in the Gospel of Jesus Christ. We must decide *immediately* where and with whom we stand in these tumultuous times.

I want to draw our attention back to the first verse of the opening hymn we sang this morning: "O young and fearless Prophet of ancient Galilee, thy life is still a summons to serve humanity; to make our thoughts and actions less prone to please the crowd, to stand with humble courage for truth with hearts uncowed."[5] Those words were penned in 1931. This is 2018. Will *our* thoughts and actions be "prone to please the crowd"? Or will we become comrades of the kin-dom?

May the courage of the prophets guide our hearts to decide. Amen.[6]

5. "O Young and Fearless Prophet." Words by S. Ralph Harlow, 1931. *The United Methodist Hymnal*, 444.

6. Commentaries consulted for this sermon included: Carvalhaes, "Commentary on Mark 6:14–29," *Working Preacher*, and Powery, "Commentary on Mark 6:14–29," *Working Preacher*.

11

God's Kingdom at the Border

Mark 10:14–15

—MICHAEL W. WATERS

I n each of the Synoptic Gospels of Matthew, Mark, and Luke, there appears a narrative of parents bringing their young children to Jesus so that Jesus might bless them. In the oldest Gospel account, the Markan Gospel, this narrative nestles between two other narratives. The first depicts Jesus as he provides instruction on marriage and divorce. The second, depicts Jesus as he presents the path to inherit eternal life. In this short and thrice repeated narrative, tension arises immediately as Jesus' own disciples vehemently oppose the proposed action of Jesus having audience with these children, castigating all who would dare to trouble the Christ with these uninvited and youthful guests.

Offering a stern rebuke of his disciples for their inhospitable response to these children, and, subsequently, to their parents as well, Jesus said, "Let the little children come to me, and do not hinder them, for the kingdom of God belongs to such as these. Truly I tell you, anyone who will not receive the kingdom of God like a little child will never enter it"(Mark 10:14–15 NRSV). The tension in the text soon abates as Jesus then embraced each child, placed his holy hands upon them and blessed each one of them, per the best intentions of their parents who brought them. In each one of these three Gospel narratives, Jesus not only showers radical hospitality upon these children, but Jesus makes these children's experience authoritative, even above his own disciples. These children become recipients of no less than the Kingdom of God, and their witness provides a primer to all who would faithfully follow their example for how to gain full access to the Kingdom of God.

When considering this well-known Gospel narrative which illuminates a clear Christological preference with regards to children, there are questions that can be and that should be raised while engaging these texts. Were Jesus' rebuke of his own disciples and strong defense of these children born exclusively out of his own moral leanings and perceptions of justice, or is its genesis found elsewhere?

Like most things Biblically considered, these questions stand open to debate. Still, when considering Jesus' own childhood experiences, and the related trauma surely accompanying those experiences, not only for Jesus, but for his entire community, one could well argue that Jesus' overwhelming sensitivity of the needs and experiences of children was born out of his own experience as a refugee child fleeing from the unspeakable violence raging in his own homeland.

Today, debates rage nationwide over the thousands of Central American children and their families who have made odyssey to the United States' southern border while fleeing the violence that has claimed so many lives—yes, even the lives of children—in their home countries. What should be done with these children, and, in many cases, the families that brought them? Should they be granted asylum in our nation, should they be detained by our nation, or should they be forcefully returned to their homeland?

Regarding Christ's own experience, each Advent season, the Gospel narrative is retold of Jesus' birth. The retelling of this ancient story often centers on the miraculous: Jesus' birth from a virgin, an illuminate celestial body resting perpetually above the manger, and angels appearing in chorus to shepherds tending their sheep in the fields at night. However, often neglected in the retelling of this story is the Matthean account that The Christ was born with a bounty on his head and that a government-sanctioned infanticide of all male children under two years of age was enacted. In order to save their child's life, Joseph and Mary had to flee with Jesus from their homeland to the borderland country of Egypt. Better still, an angel of the LORD gave Joseph a slumbering vision that they must flee, and when Joseph awoke, they fled at once Matt 2:13–18). Their departure came at divine imperative.

Yes, before Jesus could even walk or talk, Jesus was a refugee, he and his family seeking safety in Egypt. Remaining in his homeland would have meant certain death. And as Jesus grew in age and in wisdom, surely, he was made aware of the threats made against him and his community in his early life and of the tragic loss of life back home among families that were unable to flee.

It cannot be overstated that for Jesus' family crossing the border into Egypt was born out of necessity. To remain at home would have meant almost certain death. And the same is true for thousands of Central Americans seeking safety and security in America today. The near certainty of death compels them to flee their homelands, and often, at a great personal cost.

The journey to America is an arduous, perilous journey. And of the thousands of Central Americans who embark upon this northward journey, the journey is most arduous and most perilous for the most vulnerable: the children, including babies in arms. These refugees face a myriad of threats and horrors en route to America. There is the threat of starvation. There is the threat of dehydration. There is the threat of sexual assault. There is the threat of amputation while train-hopping. There is the threat of disease carrying mosquitoes and bites from poisonous snakes.

Tragically, for many Central Americans, death cruelly visits them as they make their northward odyssey fleeing from death. And now, after months of difficult travel, thousands of miles by foot and train, fleeing from death at home and circumnavigating death along the way, these refugees find that America's borders are now basically closed to them. It appears as if America has forgotten the words poetically penned by Emma Lazarus in *The New Colossus, words* long inscribed upon the Statue of Liberty which has greeted millions of refugees upon their arrival at Ellis Island: "Give me your tired, your poor, your huddled masses, yearning to breathe free."

And Jesus wept.

This is a perplexing hour when national leaders and Christian leaders alike are inventing Biblical mandates for building walls to keep out children and families that are simply yearning to be free. It should be readily clear that the brown-skinned Palestinian Jew named Jesus of Nazareth has far more in common with these refugees seeking asylum than with our nation which just has a propensity for calling herself Christian. Christ stands in solidarity with the children at our southern border. Christ stands in solidarity with children from Aleppo to Chicago and all over the world who are suffering and fleeing from violence and oppression.

Mary and Joseph's baby was surrounded by violence and immersed in poverty his entire lifetime. Poverty and the threat of violence frame Jesus' birth narrative. Mary gave birth to Jesus while exposed to the elements and surrounded by animals. Jesus' first clothes were literal rags and his first bed was a feeding trough.

The Gospels are recorded with the backdrop of poverty and oppression pulsating throughout, and Jesus' earthly ministry was dedicated to improving the lot of the poor and vulnerable in our world. Some theologians argue that the Gospels reveal a divine "preferential option" for the poor and vulnerable. And tragically, Jesus' life was cut short by a brutal public lynching on a tree.

When Jesus announced the commencement of his earthly ministry, Jesus read these words from the Isaiah scroll: "The Spirit of the Lord is upon me, for he has anointed me to bring Good News to the poor. He has sent me to proclaim that captives will be released, that the blind will see, that the oppressed will be set free, and that the time of the Lord's favor has come" (Luke 4:18–19). In this perplexing hour, it is imperative that we reclaim the true Christ and the true Gospel. If we do, we will find that Christ still stands in solidarity with the poor and most vulnerable, and we will rediscover that the Gospel is only good news if it is good news for the poor and most vulnerable among us.

As America gazes southward, it appears that the very Kingdom of God has come to our borders. And since the Christ still stands in solidarity with the poor and vulnerable of our world, it appears as if Christ himself has come to our borders to seek entry. Yet, though Christ and the Kingdom of God have come to our borders, our "Christian" nation has chosen instead to lock the Christ and the Kingdom of God in cages and to give them concrete floors and foil blankets for rest. For Jakelin Ameí Rosmery Caal Maquin, a 7-year-old Guatemalan girl seeking asylum in America with her father, our "Christian" nation allowed her to die of dehydration, fever, and shock while is U.S. custody, a death the president of the American Academy of Pediatrics says was wholly preventable. For Felipe Gomez Alonzo, an 8-year-old Guatemalan boy who while detained for a week with his father, suffered from the flu and ultimately succumbed to the illness, he received inadequate treatment before being released back into detention, our "Christian" nation failed to show him the love of Christ.

America, there is blood on your hands!

Say her name! Jakelin Ameí Rosmery Caal Maquin!

Say his name! Felipe Gomez Alonzo!

And Jesus wept.

America, do not cover your eyes. America, do not plug your ears. "Were you there when they crucified my LORD?"

Can you see Jesus as he is being ripped from Mary and Joseph's arms at our border? Can you hear Jesus weeping for his mother's milk? Can you see Jesus as he is being sexually assaulted while in custody of the American border patrol? Can you see Jesus dying of dehydration while in U. S. custody? Do you hear the cries of Jesus and his family as he flees in diapers upon bare feet as we launch canisters of tear gas upon him?

LORD, have mercy! Christ, have mercy! And Jesus wept.

And Jesus still weeps at the border. We should weep, too. But America should also heed the warning of the refugee, asylum-seeking Christ now come of age. For Jesus also spoke:

> Then he will say to those at his left hand, 'You that are accursed, depart from me into the eternal fire prepared for the devil and his angels; for I was hungry and you gave me no food, I was thirsty and you gave me nothing to drink, I was a stranger and you did not welcome me, naked and you did not give me clothing, sick and in prison and you did not visit me.' Then they also will answer, 'Lord, when was it that we saw you hungry or thirsty or a stranger or naked or sick or in prison, and did not take care of you?' Then he will answer them, 'Truly I tell you, just as you did not do it to one of the least of these, you did not do it to me.' And these will go away into eternal punishment, but the righteous into eternal life. (Matt 25:41–46)

Several years ago, America was swept away by the question made acronym "What would Jesus do?" When it comes to the Kingdom of God at our border, we need not question what Jesus would do. We simply need to remember what Jesus has already done.

Jesus would do for the refugee children of Central America and their families what he did for the "uninvited" children brought to him two millennia ago. Jesus would rebuke all—yes, even his own disciples—seeking to block these children from safety and security. Then Jesus would embrace the children, lay his holy hands upon them, and bless them with the blessings of hospitality and welcome.

131

Christ's mandate to America is undeniably clear three times over; "Let the little children come to me, and do not hinder them, for the kingdom of God belongs to such as these. Truly I tell you, anyone who will not receive the kingdom of God like a little child will never enter it" (Mark 10:14–15, NRSV).

A prominent pastor in Dallas stated in a national interview that the children of Central America should not be allowed to cross over the U.S. border. He also stated in that interview that Jesus would support his position. That's not the Gospel. That's not good news but fake news. Given that Jesus himself was as a refugee, supporting this pastor's position would make Jesus one of the biggest hypocrites in recent memory.

Thankfully, the children are still pointing the way to the Kingdom. In anticipation of a large group of child refugees' arrival in Dallas, the children's ministry at my church decided to write letters of welcome in Spanish that were delivered to some of the refugees. Through these children's witness, the truth of Scripture was once again fulfilled. Not only did they welcome these child refugees. They welcomed Jesus himself.

Truly the Kingdom of God belongs to such as these. America would do well to follow the children's example.

Amen.

12

Wounded Enough for Someone to Believe

John 20:24–28

—Heidi Neumark

²⁴ But Thomas (who was called the Twin), one of the twelve, was not with them when Jesus came. ²⁵ So the other disciples told him, "We have seen the Lord." But he said to them, "Unless I see the mark of the nails in his hands and put my finger in the mark of the nails and my hand in his side, I will not believe."

²⁶ A week later his disciples were again in the house, and Thomas was with them. Although the doors were shut, Jesus came and stood among them and said, "Peace be with you." ²⁷ Then he said to Thomas, "Put your finger here and see my hands. Reach out your hand and put it in my side. Do not doubt but believe." ²⁸ Thomas answered him, "My Lord and my God!"

I was here last year and participated in a worship service with the border church here in Tijuana. When it was time to share the peace, something odd happened. The peace was shared using only pinkie fingers. I thought this was odd and I wondered why it was done that way. After it was over, I asked about it and was told this story. It used to be that people from the Mexican side of the border and the United States side of the border could meet there in Friendship Park once a week for picnics and friendship.

Then our country built a wall, but it had slats and you could walk up to it and talk, hold hands or stroke a loved one's cheek. You could pass food, books, letters, clothing and small gifts from one side to another. It was better than nothing. Then our country built another wall in front of the first wall, with little mesh holes about the size of a Cheerio, not big enough to pass anything or stroke the face or hold the hand of a loved one. Just big enough for people to press their pinkies together in what they called a fingertip kiss. But then our country built another wall and now you can't even do that. There's a no-man's land between the two walls and people are kept so far apart you can't even wave at one another.

So now, every week, when it comes time to share the peace, the border church, meeting simultaneously on both sides, uses their pinkies to remember how it used to be. For me, it also felt like a way to recall the power and importance of every connection we can make across all the prejudices, structures and systems that would keep us apart while we also work to dismantle those walls and structures. It reminded me how even small connections, little ways we can touch each other's lives are important. Such connections can offer encouragement for the days and months ahead. After all, the life-giving, world-changing, love-and-justice-making, wall-breaking power of Jesus, comes to us in just a small piece of bread.

The last time I was in Tijuana I experienced such a connection when I met Jesus making pupusas. Ana is from El Salvador where she worked in a restaurant preparing this specialty. If you have not had the joy of eating pupusas, they are thick cornmeal flatbread stuffed with cheese, meat or beans. Ana's boss went away for a time and left her in charge of the restaurant. Before long, a gang was holding a gun to her head and demanding that she pay $500 a month, a common form of extortion. Ana explained that she was not the real owner and couldn't pay them, but they didn't believe her. Before leaving, they shot Ana in the upper arm and warned that next time it would be the head. Ana fled within days. She didn't even go to say good-bye to her 20-year-old son because she feared it would endanger his life.

When I met Ana, she was waiting in Tijuana to present herself for asylum. While she was in a shelter, she received meals through the World Central Kitchen, a wonderful "Chefs Without Borders" organization. She soon offered to volunteer, and they recognized her culinary gifts and gave her a job. I met her when I visited for a day and eventually had trouble keeping up with the pace of prepping over a thousand meals. Ana invited me to sit with her as she showed me her method of folding napkins around spoons. While we worked, she shared her story and then paused to roll up he shirt and show me the wound where the gang's bullet entered her arm. Did I think it was big enough? Noticeable enough?

She was hoping the scar will prove her case when she went for her "credible fear interview"—where asylum seekers try to convince people who are not likely to believe them or care that their life is in danger and it is not safe for them to return to their country of origin. Lacking police reports or other supporting evidence, asylum-seekers I met were hoping to offer their scarred bodies as testimony. *Put your finger here in my wound and see my hands,* says Jesus. *Reach out your hand and put it in my side. Do not doubt but believe.* But many do not believe and do not care, and asylum seekers are being sent back to their deaths. After spending a day with Ana, it was clear that she was not doing the work only for the money. I saw a woman engaged in defiant resistance, refusing to be objectified by pity or dehumanized as a criminal.

Like Jesus, in the face of betrayal, Ana took bread. In the face of suffering, Ana rose at dawn to bake bread to feed the hungry, hurting multitudes. With her wounded arms, she held out life and nourished hope. Where did she find the strength? Where do we find the strength in the face of so much hatred and evil, represented by this cold, steel wall? When we can readily feel over-powered, out-numbered and out-financed. But the Word of God is more powerful than demonic commands to create more walls. Jesus crossed the *frontera* of heaven and earth and came right through the wall, bearing his scars. He still does. *Put your finger here in my wound and see my hands. see my wounded arms says Jesus Do not doubt but believe.* Last time I was in Tijuana I met Jesus making pupusas. Amen

(Editor's Note: This sermon was preached at the border between San Diego, California, and Tijuana, Mexico.)

13

Immigrant Ministry through Relationships

—RHONDA THOMPSON

The Nehemiah Center is a Christian Community Development Program of First Baptist Church of Montgomery, Alabama Community Ministries. We serve at-risk children and families in a transitional, poverty-stricken area in Montgomery known as the Chisholm community. In 1988 Jane Ferguson was called to be the Minister of Community Ministries for First Baptist Church. Her call was to create a comprehensive ministry to help meet the physical, spiritual, emotional, and tactical needs of Montgomery's most vulnerable people. First Baptist Church Community Ministries became the premier Community Ministries program and to this day serves as a model program to churches throughout the world.

In 2000 the Community Ministries decided to go directly into the Chisholm area to meet the needs of this varied community. Ferguson recognized that the neighborhood was experiencing a great transition. This is where my ministry begins. I was given the opportunity to create a program specifically developed to meet the needs of this ever-changing neighborhood. In the words of Ferguson, I was given the charge to "go create your own program." There were three requirements. First, I was to develop a parenting program; secondly, I was to develop an after-school program for children; and finally, the challenge of a lifetime: I was to "take the ball and run with it"!

We chose the name Nehemiah Center because of the parallel to the destruction of Jerusalem and Nehemiah's charge from God to rebuild a broken city. The Chisholm community has faced the turmoil and brokenness that comes from years of neglect, poverty, and racism. Our challenge was to rebuild, reconnect, and reassure the community that there is hope. We chose to use the model of Christian Community Development. Our goal is to equip and empower people with the skills that were needed to improve their own community. Our mission statement is "Meeting human needs in the name of Jesus". Our main tool for initiating this change is relationship ministry. The Nehemiah Center is also a ministry of reconciliation. I believe that it is essential for effective ministry that we all come from a place of recognition that we have all "sinned and come short of the glory of the Lord" and that we have all been reconciled through Christ. When we truly grasp this notion, we will be continually mindful that we are all in the same boat. We may have different faults, shortcomings, or sins, but we are all dependents and beneficiaries of the salvation of Christ. As much as we like to place a human hierarchy on sin, all sins separate us from God. In order to have a life-changing relationship with those to whom we seek to minister we must not "look at the speck of sawdust in your brother's eye and pay no attention to the plank in your own eye" (Matt 7:3).

When the Nehemiah Center first began its work, the community was in a rapid transition racially and economically. The Chisholm community became composed almost exclusively of Black families. Racial reconciliation became primarily an effort of helping people outside of the community to reconcile with the needs of a community that had been left behind and suffering from a post Jim Crow era. Meeting human needs in the name of Jesus not only meant meeting the physical, emotional, and spiritual needs of the people in the community, but also bringing those outside of the community to a better understanding of racism, poverty, and the social injustices that led them to their plight. It also meant bringing myself to a place where I once again had to ask "'Lord, what is my role in the healing of this community? What would you have me learn from these people? And what might I be doing to perpetuate the difficulties that the people I have come to love so much face each day?" I know that with effective ministry with minorities, people of other races, and differing socioeconomic backgrounds comes the necessity for self-reflection of our own preconceived notions of social structures.

By 2012, the Nehemiah Center had grown into a holistic ministry providing a multitude of services for the Chisholm community including, adult education, jobs readiness, parenting classes, mental health services, housing programs, and a job placement program. Our children's program includes an after-school program, full-day summer program, tutoring program, sports programs, arts programs, and even a "chicken ministry" just to name a few. However, we began to see a rapid shift in demographics. A large group of Latino families started moving into the neighborhood. This change caused many past issues such as racial tensions and fears to resurface.

Just like in previous years, as the community changed so did our desires to reach this new people group. My prayer as director of the Nehemiah Center has always been "Lord send us the people who need us the most". Again, we continued to implement the tools of Christian Community Development and looked for partners in the community that were working with this population. This time, however, there were no others and we realized we would have to be the ones to develop the resources. Eventually, Spanish speaking churches started to appear outside of the Chisholm community. We partnered with them on several outreach events but had little success in getting the people in our area to engage. It was apparent to me that trust was a huge issue. I had been through this before when our community was transitioning from White to Black. We had worked hard in the past to build relationships with our new residents. Years of mistreatment, broken promises, and people with good intentions but shallow commitments left reasonable doubts and suspicions that we would be different. It took years of personal relationship-building to restore their trust and prove that our intentions were altruistic and that our goal was literally to share the life-changing love of God by being the hands and feet of Christ. The challenge of reaching our new Latino neighbors would be no different.

The journey was not easy. The fear of our Latino residents was real, and for good reason. The Latino community was very closed. They tried hard to stay hidden. They were very reserved and reluctant to come outside of their close familial structures. Despite our efforts to be inclusive, the barriers of language, culture, and skepticism of our intentions dampened our efforts. Several years of prayerful, intentional, and deliberate attempts to build a bridge to our new neighbors showed little success. I was aware that there was a large population of Mixtec rapidly moving into neighborhood. There was little known about this group. In an effort to understand these people, I tried to learn everything I could about them.

I began to piece together information about the history and culture of the Mixtec. As a social scientist, I was intrigued by this ancient culture that has changed so little through time. What I learned has led to a life-changing adventure in ministry.

Mixtec are an indigenous people of Mexico. Their culture and belief system are very closely related to the ancient Incas and Mayans. Even in Mexico, they are a very isolated and closed society. The Mixtec that we work with in Montgomery are primarily from the Oaxaca and Guerrero regions of Mexico. This is a very mountainous area. Mixtec are often referred to as the "people of the cloud" or "people of the corn" because they live high in the hard to reach mountains and corn is their primary crop that sustains them. The Mixtec are low on the social ladder of Mexicans. Because of their beliefs and ancient cultural practices, they are often looked down upon and discriminated against by their fellow Mexicans. The Mexican government implemented laws much like the Jim Crow laws of the southern United States. These laws were directed specifically toward the Mixtec. As a result, education, wealth, and exposure to equal opportunity has been stifled for them.

For a general overview, Mixtec are a patriarchal society. They are very family and group oriented. Individualism is not valued nor encouraged. Envy is equated with enemy in their belief system. They are a closed and fear-based society, fearing the gods, ancestors, and those "doing envy" (witchcraft). Language is a huge barrier even among Mixtec. Mixtec is an indigenous language, not a dialect. It is an ancient language and has no relation to Spanish. Names for things in the natural world are based on the hierarchy of need according to the "Mixtec Way." The language itself is limited. There are simply no words in Mixtec for many things in Spanish or English.

To understand the Mixtec, one must understand their belief system. Two of the main drivers for the Mixtec are animism and ancestralism. This controls every aspect of Mixtec life. They live almost exclusively in the spirit world believing everything that happens daily is a direct effect of the gods or the ancestors. Despite their belief in many gods, unfortunately, they have no concept of a kind and loving God who has any concern about humans. They have no concept of a God who desires a relationship with humans. Consequently, most Mixtec do not have any notion whatsoever of a God that loves them so much that He sacrificed His own Son for them. Their primary relationship to the gods is that of fear and not love.

They are ancestral. They live in constant fear that they will upset the ancestors and cause the ancestors to put a curse on them. Mixtec feel that they have no control over their daily lives. The spirits and *santos* (images of worship) control everything. The most that they can hope for is to appease the gods or ancestors so that they do not bring harm, sickness, or loss of crops to themselves.

Mixtec are in constant fear that they have not done enough or done things perfectly enough to satisfy the spirits. They believe their bodies are not fixed. They believe that they have an animal alter-ego. *Brujo/bruja* (witches) may cast evil spells on the alter-ego animal which cause sickness or injury to the person. These spirits must be appeased by sacrifice or other rituals. These spirts must be obeyed. If these spirits are not obeyed, they can cause earthquakes, famine, or other disasters. Mixtec believe that sickness is caused by the spirits. Sickness is seen as a punishment by the spirits caused by a curse from someone "doing envy". Because sickness is caused by the spirits, Mixtec will go to the local *Bruja* for treatment to drive away or reverse the spell or punishment. Their understanding is that the symptom is the disease. If the symptom is gone, then the disease is gone.

Another major influence of everyday life is the strongly held notion of the Mixtec Way. Every part of their social norms is dictated by it including what to eat, when and how to plant, when and how to celebrate, who and how to marry. Any variance from the Mixtec Way can cause the supernatural world to react. Therefore, for the Mixtec, change is bad and will only cause to make things worse. No one wants to be responsible for bringing change and causing grief from the spirits. All values and beliefs stem from the Mixtec Way. The Mixtec Way can also create a mammoth generation gap between elders from Mexico and first-generation Mixtec-Americans.

The notion of Limited Good is dominant in the Mixtec belief system. Their understanding of Limited Good is that there is a limited or finite amount of good in the world. If one receives more than their share of good, they are taking good from someone else. If one person has more than their share of good that means their neighbor has less. This good can come in the form of tangible good such as money or material things or in the form of the intangible good such as opportunity or education. This concept contributes to great secrecy within families and the community. Mixtec are not likely to share good fortune with others because they do not want to be seen as having more than their share. Envy and hatred for those that have more can cause curses and evil to happen to the person receiving more than their share. If one seeks to reach out to the Mixtec, a basic knowledge of their world view is critical.

Ministry is a journey; therefore, thinking outside of the box has been a staple in my ministry at the Nehemiah Center. The words "because we have always done it this way" seldom cross my lips. Tweaking old ideas or creating new ministry opportunities is a continual goal. Even though certain principles of Christian Community Development are steadfast, I am frequently amazed at how God can use different kinds of people and circumstances to achieve incredible outcomes. One such example is my precious little dog, Brodie. Nine years ago, Brodie and I went through the Alabama Therapy Dog certification process. After almost a year of training and preparation, Brodie was certified as a Therapy Dog with Dogs on Call. This opened a whole new avenue of ministry. One of our first long term gigs was to participants in Read-to-the-Paw. My ongoing partnership with the local schools in the area allowed me to go once a week to read to, and with, the second graders in a neighboring school. Many of the children in our children's program attended the school. The teacher had five Latino students who spoke English as their second language. They were very bright but often struggled with reading comprehension.

One of the Latino boys chosen was a Mixtec boy we will refer to as Rico. A special bond and trust were forged with Rico through our weekly visits. Brodie and I always brought goodies to class. For each holiday we would send home special treats and included would be a card with Brodie dressed for the occasion. Each card would be inscribed with a Bible verse and end with 'Love Brodie, Ms. Rhonda and the Nehemiah Center'. These messages of love would enter each home through the students. As a result, that summer we registered our first thirty Latino children, most of whom were Mixtec, for the Summer Program. After years of trying, this lovable, nine pound, four-legged, furry missionary did something that we had not been able to do before. We were able to earn the trust of five Latino families. By consistently coming each week to help their children with their reading and asking nothing in return, we were able to deliver a measurable gift of love. This was not a quick return on my investment but was a critical period of the foundation of relationship-building.

In the course of working with the Mixtec children I became increasingly aware of needs many of which were directly related to their position as immigrants. Communication is almost always a struggle for the Mixtec. Doctor visits, school interactions, things involving the government, paperwork coming through the mail that deals with daily life issues all become almost insurmountable hurtles. Helping families with these tasks became an invaluable ministry tool. The children became a direct link to building relationships with their parents. We developed programs to meet the needs of the adults including English as a Second Language classes, General Education Diploma (GED) classes for Spanish speakers, workshops and individual assistance with immigration issues, and a community garden that provided a needed connection to the earth as well as self-sufficiency.

Visiting in Rico's home became a regular treat. I was often asked to come explain a letter that had come through the mail or asked advice for doing simple tasks like addressing an envelope or buying a stamp. Coming to the home was my way of building a relation of trust with a family that had so many reasons to distrust. Each visit represented a chip being chiseled away from an existence of fear and inferiority that bound them to the chains of beliefs that kept them from experiencing freedom from the dark spirit world. I was told by some of my missionary friends that if you were ever allowed in the home of a Mixtec family, it was considered an honor. If you were ever asked to come for a meal, you were considered family for life. I was overjoyed on the day my daughter, who also works by my side with the Mixtec, and I were invited to the home for pozole or "hominies". This is an ancient soup made from hominy (a corn product) used for generations in celebrations, family gatherings, and special events. For "people of the corn" pozole is more than just a delicious food. It is seen as a link to their spiritual and ancestral connection. This trust was earned by being the hands and feet of Jesus, for loving and having an appreciation for this family where they were and for who they were.

Eventually Rico and his older brother made a profession of faith and wanted to be baptized. This was an enormous step for a Mixtec. The decision to follow the teachings of Jesus Christ meant not following the Mixtec Way. It had implications that would affect the whole family, even the whole community. This would be the first Mixtec baptism, to my knowledge, for this new community of Mixtec in Montgomery. I knew that by allowing her sons to make a public profession of faith through baptism, their mother, whom we will call Maria, and her sons where saying to the entire community that they were willing to stand up to the wrath that would follow. By choosing to turn away from the ancestors, the gods, and the tightly held communal norms that in their minds protected them from the evils of the spirit world, they would certainly be blamed for unleashing the evil that would soon follow. It was clear that Maria struggled with this decision. At one point she said that in her culture it was considered "bad luck" for someone to be baptized, and I knew what she meant by this. Approaching her concerns from a perspective of acknowledging her dark understanding of the spirit world, my response was empathetic. I shared that I believe in a God that is all powerful. My God is bigger and stronger than any evil spirit. My God has so much love for me and her that my God was willing to sacrifice God's only Son so that we could live a life filled with love and hope and not fear. Just days later, Rico and his brother were baptized.

A few weeks later Rico's mother called to say he was not feeling well. Maria had taken him to the clinic the day before and they said he most likely sprained his ankle playing soccer with his brothers. He was clearly in pain and had a slight fever. I suggested she take him back to the clinic for a follow up visit. For the next five days I would return to the home to check on Rico. At each visit his condition had worsened. Each time the family would ask my advice for a homeopathic treatment, and each time I insisted that this was more than a sprain and they should take him back to the clinic. On the next visit I told Maria that if she did not take him the next day that I would take him myself. Maria took him that day. After a very brief look at Rico, the doctor sent him in an ambulance across the street to the hospital where he was immediately put in the medical heli-copter and transferred to the Children's Hospital in Birmingham. During this entire process the medical personnel were fighting for Rico's life. He had severe septicemia and was on the verge of death. Upon arrival he went into his first surgery to save his life. The second surgery was to try to save his leg. The third surgery was to remove part of his bone, in an attempt to control the spread of the bacteria.

I have learned that nothing is easy for the Mixtec. Even joy is com-plicated with the notion of "doing envy", but when tragedy strikes, their misfortune is magnified. The spirit world is invoked in every aspect of their understanding of nature. The entire community is involved with judgment and inquiry as to who upset the gods or who went against the Mixtec Way and deserves to have the wrath of the ancestors. I knew that Maria was not only concerned for Rico but was surely entangled in the dark web of the spirit world's hold on Mixtec perception.

I later drove Maria to Children's Hospital to visit with Rico. Another family member was staying with Rico in his room, not just because he was a child, but because it was necessary that someone be with him at all times to keep even more evil spirits away. Maria was taking a chance on being around him because she was expecting another child soon. It was far too

risky for her to be around Rico for fear that whatever evil spirit was causing Rico's illness could transfer itself to the vulnerable child in her womb.
While traveling, I asked her why she waited so long to go back to the clinic
the second time. Did she just not understand how serious this could be?
Her answer was familiar. She told me that when she went the first time
there were many Mixtec people there at the clinic. They kept looking at
her and Rico and trying to figure out what was going on. She said, "I know
that they talk." She reluctantly went on to explain that if they thought
something was wrong with Rico then she would be blamed. She had not
even told her own mother about Rico's illness for the same reasons. She
knew that her mother would be angry with her for doing something that
could cause such retaliation of the spirits. She did not send the children to
the Nehemiah Center that day because she was afraid that they would say
something to one of the other Mixtec children and they would pass along
this incriminating information to their families. She had heard that we
had prayed for Rico with all of the Nehemiah Center children the day before. By doing this we uncovered a secret that she had desperately tried to
hide. Always living in fear, Maria was exercising what little control she felt
she had to limit the harm that she was certain would come. Her behavior
was not neglectful. Rather she was negotiating between what the Western
world was trying to convince her of, versus what she felt she knew based
on what the Mixtec tradition had taught her.

I asked Maria if she understood what sepsis meant. I tried to explain
as simply as I could about his condition stressing that doctors seldom
know exactly how it is contracted. Again, attempting to ease her guilt and
impose a more Christian/Western based ideology, I reminded her that
she nor Rico had done anything to cause this illness, and the doctors had
assured me that this could happen at any time to anyone. Her response
was telling. She said the doctors could not explain it to her, but she had an
explanation. She went on to give me her perception. When Rico was playing in the creek a few days earlier, the spirits entered his body through the
water. She clarified that this is a common way for spirits to enter humans
in her culture. She believed that they then got into his blood and had
spread their poison throughout his body.

Rico survived and his leg was saved. He endured more surgeries, and to
this day he still has pain and physical repercussions. Like most of my ministerial experiences, I still have more questions than answers, but I have gained
valuable lessons that has enriched my life and ministry. One important

lesson is that we may not always have the answers for those to whom we seek to minister. When ministering to immigrants and those with belief systems, cultural differences, and languages that are beyond our comprehension, we need to focus on loving them over changing them. As believers in Christ we need only to look to 1 Corinthians to understand the depth and power of love. When we love as Christ loved us, we can let go of our own understanding and lean on God's understanding. We can be the hands and feet of Christ, but we must rely on God's Holy Spirit to speak in a voice that each of God's creations can understand. I have called out to God and admitted that I am in over my head. How can I change the hearts and minds of people who have had the fears and restraints of the dark spirit world chiseled into their hearts and minds for generations? How can I communicate complex theologies in their heart language that I cannot master? The answer that I hear is this: I do not have to. I have to be reminded to heed my own teachings. I serve a God who is all powerful and is strong enough to conquer all evil. This God gives me so much love that I cannot keep it to myself. It is this God that has the power to do what I cannot do.

I share the story of Rico because it is a microcosm of my ministry with immigrants. I build on the successes, learn from my mistakes, and give value to both. Looking back on my earlier investment, I can see that the knowledge I collected about Rico's culture proved to be invaluable. Understanding their thought processes opened the door for me to pinpoint my responses in such a way as to give them more clarity and offer my counter explanations into the insight of God. Knowing that they consider themselves undeserving, trapped in fate, fear-driven, and miniscule to God led me to focus on sharing my perception of God as all powerful, kind, loving, a sacrificial giver, who calls us to love. Building relationships with Rico and his family by helping with daily struggles brought on by language barriers and lack of understanding of twenty-first century Western norms, enabled me to not only help the family with the tasks at hand, but in doing so I earned their trust and respect. This trust and respect gave way to openness of my beliefs and insight. Taking the time to go to doctors' appointments, school interventions, drug stores, helping with municipal obligations and more, also bridged a gap between this misunderstood and isolated people group and the community that needed more understanding of them. As the connector, I became a sought-after advisor to both groups. The same people who I sought for help were now seeking my help. As a result, I was able to help shape both world views. By facilitating both parties, my Christlike influence was mutual.

My mistakes were many, but I will always rely on what I have learned from them. I respect their privacy even when I have the impulse to spread good news, share concerns, pray publicly, or give openly. I acknowledge that unintended consequences may bring harm or undue grief. When we prayed as a group for Rico it felt good to me. I felt comforted, empowered, and secure in God's ability to bring healing. This proved to be on my timeline not Maria's. My desire to unite a community in support translated into a nightmare for Maria. Like all ministry, we must shape our strategies to fit the people we wish to serve, not shape the people to fit out strategy. Maria and her family have helped me learn my limits. I have been a social worker for almost thirty years and the lines are seldom clear. I do know that we are called to give of ourselves sacrificially. We are called to step out of our comfort zone, learn new things, and accept that we do not have all the answers. I have a greater understanding for the power of evil, yet I have an even stronger respect for the power of God's love to conquer things that I cannot change.

Mindful of this, I rely on a few basic ministerial and Christian Community Development principles that relate to all people groups especially our immigrants. We must meet people where they are. We need to value them as they are without imposing our judgment on them. We can do this by recognizing that we are all reconciled through Christ, each having our own shortcomings, and each depending on Christ for our salvation. Our first step in reaching out to them is to build a relationship of trust. This comes with time, altruistic service, and perseverance. Any motive other than sharing the unconditional love of God will be exposed in time for what it is. It is our responsibility as servants to attempt to understand their culture and belief systems. By doing this we show them that they are important to us, that we recognize value in their culture, and we recognize their value to God. It is necessary to listen to their story from their words in order to know them. If we gain this knowledge, then we can be a credible source of knowledge to the rest of our community by educating, building bridges, and dispelling misinformation and misunderstandings that separates immigrants from the community at large.

Developing partnerships with others serving the immigrant population is crucial as well. The Nehemiah Center works closely with our Baptist Association and has participated in a Mixtec Task Force that brings others working with the Mixtec population together for the purpose of creating strategies, sharing ideas and resources, and encouraging our fellow servants. Because of a core group of Mixtec that were already invested in the Nehemiah Center, we chose to start a Mixtec Church Plant at the Nehemiah Center. Working outside of the faith-based community is essential also. I helped form a Latino outreach organization known as HOLA, Hispanic Outreach and Leadership in Action. HOLA is housed on the Nehemiah Center Campus with a goal of empowering, educating, and equipping Latinos in the Greater Montgomery Area. We bring leaders throughout our region together to combine resources and knowledge that can improve the lives of Latinos. By being a leader in this group, I can bring a Christian perspective to a secular partnership. Schools, public agencies, and police collaborations have been critical to our immigrant ministry. Again, I have spent years building these relationships by visibly serving the people with whom I wish to unite our immigrants. I offer my assistance to them without ulterior motives and in return we have established a trust that is mutually beneficial. In cultivating these relationships, I have also been able to prove that in serving this community we are indeed serving God.

Another critical principle is that we must listen and learn. In the beginning of our Nehemiah Center ministry we did a comprehensive needs assessment. As our demographics changed so did our strategies. Focus should be placed on what the community tells us they need instead of what our perception of what their needs are. We begin with addressing their priorities and work beside them, not over them. In working side by side, we can have greater influence on our mission which is "Meeting human needs in the name of Jesus". I believe we must humble ourselves and realize that our own wealth and privilege does not equate to superiority. When we tear down our own walls of pride and arrogance, and replace them with bridges of respect and acceptance, then we can begin to embrace the richness of what God would have us learn. Listening to the experiences of the Mixtec I am often in awe of their ability to survive. The reverence they give toward their elders, the almost impenetrable devotion they have toward family, the respect they place on the natural world versus the material world, and the sacrificial generosity that they show me has certainly led to my own self-examination and spiritual growth.

As I mentioned earlier, my prayer for the Nehemiah Center has always been that the Lord will send us those who need us the most. On my first encounter with a Mixtec missionary, I soaked in all the information that I could, but what to this day stands out to me the most is a picture that he painted of the Mixtec with his words. According to the Southern Baptist International Mission Board, the Mixtec are considered the largest unreached people group in the world. This means that this is the largest group in the world that has never once been exposed to the gospel. This indigenous group that has changed so little since from their ancient Mayan ancestors, has lived for centuries just miles from the United States border. As Christians the Great Commission calls us to go into all the world and teach them about saving power of Christ Jesus. Despite our bold efforts to cross oceans, go into faraway countries, trek to reclusive areas where Westerners have seldom dared to go in order to carry out our mission, we have yet to reach the Mixtec only miles away with our Good News. Like myself, most folks in Montgomery, Alabama were totally unaware of the existence of the Mixtec people, yet I am convinced that God has literally brought them to our doorsteps. It is as if God has said, "I have been waiting on you for centuries to come to my people, and they can wait no more. I am now sending them to you." What a privilege it is be chosen by God to be the first ever to share the gospel with God's children. What an honor to be the bearers of light to the Mixtec who have lived in the darkness of the spirit world for hundreds of years. It has been the joy of my life to give hope to a community of people that have lived for generations under the suppression of despair and hopelessness. My best advice to anyone who feels the call to minister to our immigrant populations is this: do NOT let this opportunity pass you by!

14

By God's Grace

Stumbling into Multi-Cultural Ministry
and Lessons Learned

—JASON CROSBY

C rescent Hill Baptist Church in Louisville, Kentucky is a multicultural congregation primarily due to God's grace and the willingness of hundreds, if not thousands, of people to risk something big for the sake of something good over the course of two-centuries. In order to understand how multi-cultural ministry functions at Crescent Hill Baptist Church, one must begin in Salem, Massachusetts in the year 1812. After setting our multi-cultural congregation in its historical context, lessons that have been learned doing ministry in a multi-cultural congregation for nearly fifteen years are shared.

Historical Context: The Judsons

On February 19, 1812, two weeks to the day after their wedding, 23-year-old Adoniram Judson and his wife Ann set sail on a ship named the Caravan from Salem, Massachusetts, planning to go to India to serve as missionaries. When the Judsons arrived in Calcutta, tensions between the United States and Britain were running high. The British authorities who controlled Calcutta at the time refused to allow these American missionaries to enter

India. With India out of the picture, the Judsons changed their plans and decided to sail across the Bay of Bengal to Burma and serve as missionaries there. They arrived in Burma on July 13, 1813, 206 years ago.

At first, the going was difficult for the Judsons in Burma. The first three years there, the couple cut themselves off from nearly all contact with English speakers and Americans and reports say they spent twelve hours a day learning the Burmese language. The Judsons did not conduct a public Christian meeting until 1819, six years after their arrival in Burma. In 1822, the Judsons reported eighteen converts to Christianity. Then, in 1824 the first Anglo-Burmese War began. Adoniram was accused of being a British spy, was arrested, and remained in a Burmese prison for seventeen months. Eventually, Adoniram was released, but only a couple months later, Ann, died.

Judson first encountered the Karen people in 1827. Judson befriended a Karen man, Ko Tha Byu, who later became the first Karen Christian. When Judson met Ko Tha Byu, Ko Tha Byu was a slave and a convicted thief and murderer. Yet, it was Ko Tha Byu, despite his checkered past and the fact that he was illiterate, that brought the message of God's love in Jesus Christ he learned about via the Judsons to the Karen people. Judson continued to effectively minister in Burma, primarily among the Karen, until his death. In 2012, a bicentennial celebration was held to celebrate the Judsons arrival. Tens of thousands of people participated in the festivities.

"The Mother Church"

Members of Clifton Baptist Church decided to plant a new congregation further east along Frankfort Avenue in the adjacent Crescent Hill neighborhood in 1908. Crescent Hill Baptist Church constructed its first building in 1916 at the corner of Birchwood Avenue and Frankfort Avenue. In 1926, Southern Baptist Theological Seminary relocated from its then location in downtown Louisville to its current location between Lexington Road and Grinstead Avenue—less than one block from Crescent Hill Baptist Church. The congregation demolished the building it had constructed just a decade early in order to build its current sanctuary that very same year. The sanctuary served as the primary gathering space from the seminary for decades.

The geographic proximity of Crescent Hill Baptist Church and the seminary not only meant that the seminary used the church's space. It also resulted in the church serving as a spiritual home for scores of the seminary's faculty, staff, and students. The congregation's identity became intertwined with the seminary. That symbiotic relationship served both seminary and church well. However, when the seminary veered sharply to the right in the early 1990s, the mutually beneficial institutional relationship came to a screeching halt. When seminary faculty, staff, students, and their family fled from Louisville, Crescent Hill Baptist Church lost hundreds of members. Moreover, the church lost its identity and mission.

Chiang Mai, Louisville, and a New Hope

The years between end of the close relationship between the seminary and CHBC and the arrival of refugees from Burma were especially crucial. No two individuals were more invested in the events that transpired in those years than Steve Clark and Annette Ellard, who were and are CHBC members and now serve as Cooperative Baptist Fellowship Field Personnel. What follows is their recount of what unfolded at CHBC from the mid-1990s until 2007.

Steve Clark and Annette Ellard and the Work with the Karen People

On February 25, 2007, Crescent Hill Baptist Church welcomed a young woman who came to Louisville to work as an interpreter for Karen refugees from Burma. The next Sunday, the church welcomed refugees from Burma into our family for the first time. Now, twelve years later, we all are forever changed.

In 1998, the church decided to participate in the Cooperative Baptist Fellowship's "Adopt-a-People Program," choosing the Rock People (Paluang people) of Thailand. In 2000, Bill Johnson and then missions committee chair Paul Capps traveled to Thailand to visit CBF Field Personnel Rick and Ellen Burnette and learn how the church could be involved more directly in ministry with the Paluang. When Bill and Paul arrived in Chiang Mai, the Burnettes had been delayed for a few days, so they placed Bill and Paul in the care of a missionary couple from Australia to keep them occupied. While waiting for the Burnettes, Bill and Paul visited several ministry sites in Chiang Mai, including the Thailand Karen Baptist Convention (TKBC), with its Karen youth hostel located adjacent to their office.

When Bill and Paul returned and made their report to the congregation, the church was excited and wanted to schedule a team to go to Thailand in the next year, but the Burnettes could not work out a date for a mission project with CHBC until the fall of 2002. The church didn't want the enthusiasm for a missions project to wane by waiting nearly two years, so they decided to contact the ministries in Chiang Mai (where Bill and Paul had been delayed) for an opportunity to partner together for a mission project in 2001.

So, in July of 2001, Crescent Hill Baptist Church sent a team of ten who went to Chiang Mai, Thailand, for ten days to paint the youth hostel operated by the Thailand Karen Baptist Convention. Before the project, the whole church focused on learning about the Karen people, even having "Karen Sunday" when every Sunday School class studied about the Karen people and prayed for them. We were a part of that team, and this was our first contact with the Karen people. We worked together to paint the two-story dormitory with a band of Karen high school students and their house-parents.

As we worked, it became obvious to the group that the two of us were really able to communicate and form relationships with the Karen students. Our teammates asked us to spend more time in conversation while they worked harder at painting. On that first trip to Thailand we made lifelong friends with many of the students, and on later mission trips with the church in 2002 and 2004, we stayed several weeks longer than the rest of the mission teams to visit several remote villages of some of our Karen friends. God was preparing us for our future work with refugees.

In 2005, we felt God compelling us to give our lives to full time mission service and were appointed by the Cooperative Baptist Fellowship as field personnel in June of 2006. Six months later, we discovered that the first Karen families from Burma being resettled in the United States had begun to arrive in Louisville, and they were without a Karen interpreter.

We immediately arranged for Duane Binkley, the former director of the Thailand Baptist Missionary Fellowship and ABC-USA missionary to the Karen to come to Louisville to meet with refugee agencies and provide some cultural information about the Karen. We also helped to put together a meeting with potential church sponsors for KRM in its meeting with Duane. A few days after those meetings, Duane found a Karen woman to be an interpreter for Catholic Charities. We greeted her at the airport the weekend she arrived and helped her get settled in. Mary Neal Clarke, member of CHBC and retired missionary, offered the young woman a room in her home until we could find her an apartment.

Of course, we brought her to church with us to Crescent Hill to worship. After her first two days on the job, Dah Htoo, the mother of a Karen family, asked her where she went to church. The interpreter replied that she had only been in Louisville for a few days but went to church with her friends Steve and Annette and they told her that the church knew Karen people. Dah Htoo needed a good church home and asked if she could come to church with her.

On Tuesday night the interpreter asked us if it would be okay for Dah Htoo and her children to come to church with her at Crescent Hill. Of course, we said "yes," and planned to pick them up on Sunday morning. By Wednesday, Dah Htoo had told two other families that she was going with the interpreter to a church that knew Karen people, and they all asked if they could come, too. By Thursday morning, the number of Karen had increased from six to 19, and we were making plans for the CHBC church vans to pick them all up on Sunday morning for worship.

On March 4, 2007, a total of twenty Karen refugees dressed in traditional red and blue Karen clothes, were welcomed to Crescent Hill Baptist Church for the first time. Our two church vans brought Dah Htoo's family, Jelly Htoo's family and Ar Pay Moo's family to worship, along with an extra Karen man, Key Ler Ber Poe. He spent the night with one of the families in order to come to the church and see if he would like to bring his family of nine next time. The next Sunday, 28 Karen people came (with the addition of Key Ler Ber Poe's family). On the next Sunday, 35 Karen people came, and by the middle of the summer there were more than 100.

The nursery and children's classes were bursting at the seams. There were more than 25 Karen youth in the youth classes and a new adult Karen Sunday School Class was formed with Nar K'Paw and Hay Moo Law Eh as interpreters. In a matter of a few months, Crescent Hill Baptist Church became known as the church in Louisville that knew and loved Karen people, and a primary place for refugees from Burma to come together for worship and fellowship with each other and with welcoming American friends.

Lessons Learned: God Is at Work in This Realm

Crescent Hill Baptist Church did not set out to be a multi-cultural congregation. We did not launch a ministry with the intention of transforming our congregation into a multi-cultural one. However, upon looking back at the events that unfolded over centuries that resulted in our congregation becoming a multi-cultural one, the first lesson that many of us learned is that God really is at work in this realm.

God's sense of time may not square with our sense of time. Judson probably doubted God was at work in the world when after many years only a few people in Burma converted to Christianity. I know many at CHBC doubted that God was at work in the world in the wake of the conservative shift of Southern Baptist Theological Seminary when CHBC lost many resources and more importantly its congregational identity. However, the likes of the Judsons, Ko Tha Byu, Steve Clark, Annette Ellard, Dah Htoo, nursey workers at CHBC, van drivers at CHBC, and scores of others, over time it became clear that God is at work in the world. We frequently retell this story at CHBC because the path God took and the people God used to transform our congregation is a reminder that when average people do their best to faithfully do what God is asking them to do next, in time, the reign of God as it exists in heaven becomes more manifest on earth.

1. Multicultural Church is not for Everyone

The first few years of operation as a multicultural congregation were difficult. When God asks a person or a people to make a leap of faith, it usually comes at a cost. The sudden and unexpected arrival of so many new congregants from Burma upended the established culture and practices at CHBC. All of the sudden, we needed a team of drivers to assist with transportation to and from the church on both Sundays and Wednesdays. All of the sudden, we needed to find twice as many volunteers to help staff our nursery and toddler area on Sunday mornings. All of the sudden, our Children's Sunday School teachers were put in a position where they were teaching classes where children from Burma outnumbered US born children three or four to one. Furthermore, hardly any of the children from Burma or their parents spoke English even at a level that could be considered proficient. All of the sudden, we were forced to alter our established worship pattern at CHBC in order to incorporate the other languages and foreign (to us) worship expectations.

Needless to say, these sudden, dramatic shifts did not suit everyone well. Isaac Newton's Third Law of Physics states, "For every action there is an equal and opposite reaction." As dozens of new members joined the ranks of CHBC, dozens of others left the church. Interestingly, the majority of people who left the congregation during this time were families with children. Most expressed concern about their child's ability to receive adequate Christian education and attention in a place where more children spoke a language other than English. We went through a season of church membership white flight that took an emotional, spiritual, and tangible toll. Multi-cultural ministry is not for everyone.

2. Listening

Most at CHBC thought that when the Karen first showed up at the church, they would need worship space and some additional support as they settled into life in the United States. Leadership at the church at the time was surprised when those from Burma expressed a different preference. Those from Burma expressed a desire to be a part of the church. They wanted to join the church, worship with others, and give back to the larger body as best as possible. That response was very instructive for those who were already a part of the CHBC community. It informed those already established at CHBC that presumptions needed to be checked at the door and that listening would be essential moving forward.

Not long after the transformation, Imago Dei came into being. Imago Dei (the image of God) was a team that met monthly. It served as a forum where leaders from various racial and ethnic groups who were gathering at 2800 Frankfort could gather for food, informal conversation, and a chance for those who were coming from the context of the CHBC establishment to listen. Through that monthly meeting and other opportunities for listening, learning and growth, we were all enabled and empowered to better understand one another so that we could continue to live and learn and be together.

3. Giving Up Power

Often, without even noticing, congregations fall into the trap of being clubs through which power is consolidated and preserved. In fourteenth chapter of Luke's gospel, we read that Jesus gathered for a meal at an important person's home along with many other important people. They were leery of Jesus, but Jesus knew that how they approached that table, who gathered around that table, and where people sat at that table would communicate a great deal. He watched those important people carefully position themselves. I can easily picture in my mind's eye a religious leader shrewdly sitting down next to a business leader in the hopes of securing funding for the next building project. I can also imagine an educational leader taking a place next to a philanthropist in the hopes of increasing the institution's endowment. Jesus knew that the gathering around this table in this home was not merely one in which people came to satisfy their bellies. These important people carefully positioned themselves around the table in order to further their ambitions. They gathered to maintain and perhaps attain more power for themselves and their constituents. Jesus knew that if you are not at the table, you are on the menu.

After surveying this scene, Jesus said, "But when you give a banquet, invite the poor, the crippled, the lame and the blind." In other words, Jesus told those with power around that table not to keep it for themselves. Instead, power in the reign of God is equally distributed. All have a place at the table, and no one is on the menu.

Multi-cultural congregations seeking to bring the heaven close to earth are ones where those who have power—be it financial, social, or political—is given up by those who possess it for the betterment of those who do not. A congregation may be multi-cultural on the surface. People from different races and places may gather under the roof to worship. However, a multi-cultural congregation that looks like the reign of God is one where those with power divest themselves of it.

A Great Samaritan: Expanding Our Concepts of Neighbor, Charity, and Mercy

As long as people have walked the earth, people have been on the move.

Sometimes, people move voluntarily. The itch to explore new frontiers has led many a person to leave behind the familiar for the uncharted. Many people have voluntarily decided to leave behind the comfortable and stable to see the world and pursue personal and professional dreams.

The United Nations High Commission for Refugees, the world's leading organization seeking to assist displaced people reports that in 2019 more than Seventy million people have been forcibly displaced from their homes. Forty-one million people are internally displaced, which means that due to some form of persecution those individuals have been removed from their homes but remain within a nation. Almost twenty-six million people are currently classified as refugees. The rest of forcibly displaced individuals are asylum seekers.[1]

1. "Figures at a Glance." United Nations High Commission on Refugees, UNCHR.

Once upon a time I found myself in law school. One summer while in law school I worked for a federal appellate court judge. I spent most of my time in that office reviewing appeals made by asylum seekers. Asylum seekers are different than internally displaced people (IDPs) and refugees. All IDPs, refugees, and asylum seekers are migrants, but not all migrants are IDPs, refugees, or asylum seekers. There is an important distinction between these three categories. Refugees are people forced out of a country due to political, religious, or ethnic persecution. Refugees then enter a second country where they often remain in camps for years, if not decades. Eventually, a fortunate few refugee are resettled in another country. Asylum seekers are people who feel they have no choice but to leave a country. Rather than wait in a refugee camp, these individuals enter into a country like the United States in hopes that once there, they will find a safe haven. That's what many of the migrants along the United States' southern border at the moment are attempting to accomplish. What became crystal clear to me many years ago when reading through asylum seekers from Central America's stories is this . . . these people from El Salvador, Nicaragua, and Honduras did not want to come to the United States. By and large, they felt they had no choice. They feared that if they remained in their country they would die, or members of their families would be persecuted. Most people, if given the choice, would rather live out their lives in their native land. Migration is usually an involuntary act.

As long as people have been on the move, people have been struggling to figure out how to live with one another in the face of deep differences. When people move and come into proximity with others, inevitably different customs and values collide. Often times, these differences create friction and heat that generates hate.

Friction, heat, and hatred defined the relationship between the Samaritans and Jews. The tension between them began with involuntary migration. The Samaritans and Judean and Galilean Jews had been in conflict for hundreds of years. Actually, both the Samaritans and what we commonly refer to as the Jews that Jesus associated with were both practicing the Jewish faith. However, for the sake of ease of communication, I will refer to the two groups as the Samaritans and the Jews, but don't forget that these two groups shared a common religious tradition. The conflict between these two groups of people began when the Assyrians conquered much of Israel in the 8th century BCE. The Assyrians took many Israelites captive and forced others to

org, https://www.unhcr.org/en-us/figures-at-a-glance.html

157

migrate to Israelite territory. Intermarriage between the Israelites that were left in the land and non-Israelites resettled there led to the rise of the Samaritans. The Assyrians eventually lost their grip on power, but the hostility they helped create between the Samaritan and Jewish people through forced migration lasted hundreds and hundreds of years.

That conflict was simmering just beneath the surface when the lawyer approached Jesus. The lawyer asks Jesus what he must do to inherit eternal life. As I mentioned previously, I once was enrolled in law school. I do not remember much of what I learned, but I do remember this much . . . whenever a lawyer asks a question it is not just a question. It is an often-used strategic technique used to catch adversaries in a trap. Jesus understood the strategy. Jesus responds to the lawyer's question with a question. Jesus asks the lawyer a question that he can easily answer. "What does the law say?" The lawyer responds correctly. Jewish law says, "'Love the Lord your God with all your heart and with all your soul and with all your strength and with all your mind'; and, 'Love your neighbor as yourself.'" Jesus said, "go and do this, and you will live." But the lawyer is a lawyer and so naturally another question followed. "Who is my neighbor?" Does my neighbor mean just whom I associate with or live near? Or, does it include others like enemies or those in other lands?

The lawyer's question affords Jesus the perfect opportunity to use the long-running Samaritan-Jewish conflict to define who is a neighbor? The man robbed and beaten and left for dead was most likely a Jew. That road running from Jerusalem to Jericho was Jewish territory. Two fellow Jews pass by without stopping to assist. First a religious leader. Then, a Levite. It is a despised Samaritan, however, who comes to the ailing Jews' assistance. Who bandages his wounds? Who takes him to an inn where he receives additional care?

Again, Jesus responds to the lawyer's question with yet another question. Who was the robbed and beaten and left for dead man's neighbor? Jesus by way of questioning and parable outlawyered the lawyer. The lawyer was trapped. He had no choice but to acknowledge that the neighbor was the Samaritan. Everyone you encounter, even your enemy, is your neighbor who are you called to love and show mercy to. "Go," Jesus says, "and do likewise." Your neighbor is anyone you meet in need along the way. Your neighbor is especially anyone in need along the side of the road, no matter his or her race, religious practice, ethnicity or nationality.

Jesus redefined the definition of neighbor for his fellow Judean and Galilean Jews. He expanded the scope. He challenged the nativism and tribalism of his people.

He also pressed the bounds of what charity and mercy entails as well. Note that the Samaritan did not just call an ambulance or throw a few dollars towards the man.

We are told the Samaritan . . .

> Went to him and bandaged his wounds, having poured oil and wine on them. Then he put him on his own animal, brought him to an inn, and took care of him. The next day he took out two denarii, gave them to the innkeeper, and said, "Take care of him; and when I come back, I will repay you whatever more you spend."

Jesus asks us to expand who we think of as our neighbors. Jesus, via this parable, asks us to expand the way in which we think of charity and mercy. Charity and mercy are not just throwing a few coins or bills at someone who approaches us on the sidewalk. Charity and mercy are not just writing a check at a fundraising event. Charity and mercy entail that and then following up the next day, the next day, the next day, and perhaps following up the next day after that. Following worship this morning a group will meet to discuss assisting a refugee family from the Congo resettle in the United States. We are currently collecting school supplies and will be assembling them in partnership with United Crescent Hill Ministries in a couple weeks. Charity and acts of mercy are vital.

However, while we are doing this, while are contemplating the ways in which Jesus is expanding our understanding of who is our neighbor and what charity and mercy entails, we must understand the limitations of charity and mercy. We must consider the distinction between charity and mercy and justice.

In his sermon the "One Sided Approach to the Good Samaritan," Martin Luther King Jr. said,

> "But not only is it possible to elevate the roles of the Priest and Levite; it is also easy to see the shortcomings in the conduct of the Samaritan.
>
> There is no suggestion that the Samaritan sought to investigate the lack of police protection on the Jericho Road. Nor did he appeal to any public officials to set out after the robbers and clean up the Jericho road. Here was the weakness of the Good Samaritan. He was concerned with temporary relief, not with thorough

reconstruction. He sought to sooth the effects of evil, without going back to uproot the causes.

Now, without a doubt Christian social responsibility includes the sort of thing the Good Samaritan did. So, we give to the United Appeals, the Red Cross, to all types of unfortunate conditions. In the midst of such staggering and appalling conditions we cannot afford to "pass by on the other side." Like the good Samaritan we must always stand ready to descend to the depth of human need. The person who fails to look with compassion upon the thousands of individuals left wounded by life's many roadsides is not only unethical, but ungodly. Every Christian must ply the good Samaritan

But there is another aspect of Christian social responsibility which is just as compelling. It seeks to tear down unjust conditions and build anew instead of patching things up. It seeks to clear the Jericho road of its robbers as well as caring for the victims of robbery."[2]

A Good Samaritan understands anyone walking the face of this earth is neighbor. A Good Samaritan practices radical charity and mercy. The kind of charity and mercy that follows up the next day and the next day after that. A Great Samaritan does not stop there. A Great Samaritan bucks the system that makes the Jericho Road a dangerous stretch to begin with. A Great Samaritan understands the difference between charity and mercy and justice. A Great Samaritan understands that you do what you must do in the here and now to help folks along the journey, but also is working to alter the here and now so that charity and mercy will no longer be necessary. When the "kingdom" of God comes to earth as it is in heaven, there will be no need for charity and mercy. For then, all will be well. All will be just and peaceful. There will no longer be contentious borders or Jericho Roads.

Who is your neighbor? What act of charity and mercy will you do this day? How are you advocating for more just systems that will make charity and mercy unnecessary in the days to come?

2. Martin Luther King Jr., "The One-Sided Approach of the Good Samaritan."

Bibliography

Abramitzky, Ran, and Leah Boustan. "Immigration in American Economic History." *Journal of Economic Literature* 55 (2017) 1311–45. https://www.ncbi.nlm.nih.gov/pmc/articles/PMC5794227/pdf/nihms753089.pdf.

Alcoff, Linda Martín. *The Future of Whiteness*. Malden, MA: Polity, 2015.

Amnesty International Report (April 2010), http://www.amnesty.org/en/library/asset/AMR41/014/2010/en/8459f0ac-03ce-4302-8bd2-3305bdae9cde/amr410142010eng.pdf.

Anderson, Stuart. *Immigration*. Greenwood Guides to Business and Economics. Santa Barbara, CA: Greenwood, 2010.

Ayala, César J., and Rafael Bernabe. *Puerto Rico in the American Century: A History since 1898*. Chapel Hill: University of North Carolina Press, 2007.

Bailey, Clinton. *Bedouin Poetry from Sinai to the Negev: Mirror of a Culture*. Oxford: Clarendon, 1991.

Baker, Bryan. *Estimates of the Illegal Alien Population Residing in the United States: January 2015*. United States Department of Homeland Security: Office of Immigration Statistics (December 2018). https://www.dhs.gov/sites/default/files/publications/18_1214_PLCY_pops-est-report.pdf.

Barrionuevo, Alexei. "Mountains of Corn and a Sea of Farm Subsidies." *New York Times*, November 9, 2005.

Bartow, Charles L. *God's Human Speech: A Practical Theology of Proclamation*. Grand Rapids: Eerdmans, 1997.

Bello, Walden. "The World Bank, the IMF, and the Multinationals: Manufacturing the World Food Crises." *The Nation*, June 8, 2008.

Betz, Hans Dieter. *The Sermon on the Mount*. Hermeneia. Minneapolis: Fortress, 1995.

Bier, David. "U.S. Approves Far Fewer Muslim Refugees, Immigrants, & Travelers." Last updated Apr. 23, 2018. https://www.cato.org/blog/us-approves-far-fewer-muslim-refugees-immigrants-travelers.

Black, Kathy. *A Healing Homiletic: Preaching and Disability*. Nashville: Abingdon, 1996.

Bonhoeffer, Dietrich. *Ethics*. Translated by Reinhard Kraus et al. Dietrich Bonhoeffer Works 6. Minneapolis: Fortress, 2005.

Bright, John. *A History of Israel*. 4th ed. Louisville: Westminster John Knox, 2000.

Brueggemann, Walter. *Cadences of Home: Preaching among Exiles*. Louisville: Westminster John Knox, 1997.

———. *The Land*. 2nd ed. Overtures to Biblical Theology. Minneapolis: Fortress, 2002.

Carranza, Rafael. "Four Aid Volunteers Found Guilty of Dropping Off Water, Food for Migrants in Arizona Desert." *Arizona Republic*, January 20, 2019. https://www.usatoday.com/story/news/nation/2019/01/20/volunteers-guilty-dropping-water-food-migrants-arizona-desert/2632435002/

Carvalhaes, Cláudio. "Commentary on Mark 6:14–29." *Working Preacher*, July 15, 2018. https://www.workingpreacher.org/preaching.aspx?commentary_id=3736

Chapman, Michael W. "CIA Dir. Pompeo: 'Jesus Christ Our Savior Is Truly the Only Solution for Our World.'" CNS News, Jan. 25, 2017. https://www.cnsnews.com/news/article/michael-w-chapman/cia-dir-pompeo-jesus-christ-our-savior-truly-only-solution-our-world

Connor, Phillip. "U.S. Admits Record Number of Muslim Refugees in 2016." Last updated Oct. 5, 2016. http://www.pewresearch.org/fact-tank/2016/10/05/u-s-admits-record-number-of-muslim-refugees-in-2016.

Davies, W. D. *The Sermon on the Mount*. Cambridge: Cambridge University Press, 1990.

De La Torre. Miguel A. *Reading the Bible from the Margins*. Maryknoll, NY: Orbis, 2002.

———. *Trails of Hope and Terror: Testimonies on Immigration*. Maryknoll, NY: Orbis, 2009.

Delgadillo, Theresa. *Spiritual Mestizaje: Religion, Gender, Race, and Nation in Contemporary Chicana Narrative*. Latin America Otherwise. Durham: Duke University Press, 2011.

Department of Homeland Security. DHS Organizational Chart. https://www.dhs.gov/xlibrary/assets/dhs-orgchart.pdf.

Dillen, Annemie. "Good News for Children? Towards a Biblical Hermeneutic of Texts of Terror." *Irish Theological Quarterly* 76 (2011) 164–82.

Du Bois, W. E. B. *The Souls of White Folk*. In *Writings*. New York: Library of America, 1986.

Ehrkamp, Patricia, and Caroline Nagel. "'Under the Radar': Undocumented Immigrants, Christian Faith Communities, and the Precarious Spaces of Welcome in the U.S. South." *Annals of the Association of American Geographers* 104 (2014) 319–28.

Eichenwald, Kurt. "Borderline Insanity." *Newsweek Global* 165.15 (October 23, 2015) 26–33.

Eustáquio de Souza, Geraldo. "Geraldo Eustáquio de Souza: Desistir . . . eu já pensei seriamente . . ." *Pensador* (website). https://www.pensador.com/frase/MTAwMTQzMA/.

Ewing, Walter A. "Opportunity and Exclusion: A Brief History of U.S. Immigration Policy." American Immigration Council, http://www.immigrationpolicy.org/sites/default/files/docs/opportunity_exclusion_011312.pdf/.

Feldman, Stephen M. *Please Don't Wish Me a Merry Christmas: A Critical History of the Separation of Church and State*. New York: New York University Press, 1997.

Fernández, Manny. "'You Have to Pay with Your Body': The Hidden Nightmare of Sexual Violence on the Border." *The New York Times*, March 3, 2019. https://www.nytimes.com/2019/03/03/us/border-rapes-migrant-women.html

Gowan, Donald E. "Wealth and Poverty in the Old Testament: Care of the Widow, the Orphan, and the Sojourner." *Interpretation*. 41 (1984) 341–53.

Grace United Methodist Church. Homepage. "Welcome to Grace Church." https://www.graceumcdallas.org.

Green, Emma. "Trump Creates a not-so-new Faith Office in the White House." *The Atlantic,* May 3, 2018. https://www.theatlantic.com/politics/archive/2018/05/trump-creates-a-not-so-new-faith-office-in-the-white-house/559574.

Guardiola-Sáenz, Leticia, "Border-crossing and Its Redemptive Power in John 7:53—8:11: A Cultural Reading of Jesus and the Accused." In *John and Postcolonialism: Travel, Space, and Power,* edited by by Musa W. Dube and Jeffrey L. Staley, 267–91. Sheffield: Sheffield Academic, 2002.

Guelich, Robert A. *The Sermon on the Mount: A Foundation for Understanding.* Waco, TX: Word, 1982.

Guyjoco, Chiqui. "Cardinal Vincent Nichols Condemns 'Upsurge' of Racism and Hatred in Brexit Aftermath." *The Christian Times.* July 1, 2016. http://christiantimes.com/article/cardinal-vincent-nichols-condemns-brexits-upsurge-of-racism-and-hatred/58037.htm.

Hanson, Paul D. *A People Called: The Growth of Community in the Bible.* San Francisco: Harper & Row, 1986.

Haynes, Elosia P. "Mixed-Status Families and the Threat of Deportation." *Journal of Sociology & Social Welfare* 44 (2017) 99–118.

Herman, Judith Lewis *Trauma and Recovery: The Aftermath of Violence – From Domestic Abuse to Political Terror.* New York: Basic Books, 1997.

Hing, Julianne. "Who Would Win an Immigration Debate between Sanders and Clinton? Martin O'Malley." *Nation,* November 3, 2015.

Hollinger, David. *After Cloven Tongues of Fire: Protestant Liberalism in Modern American History.* Princeton: Princeton University Press, 2013.

Hong, Kari. "Weaponizing Misery: The 20-Year Attack on Asylum." 22 *Lewis & Clark Law Review* 541 (2018) 541–76.

Hope, Lori. "Did I Save Lives or Engage in Profiling?" *Newsweek,* March 31, 2002. https://www.newsweek.com/did-i-save-lives-or-engage-profiling-141445.

Howard, Melanie A. "Paradigm of Peace, Silly Satire, Text of Terror: Perspectives on Matthew 5:38–48 for Immigrant Populations." *Soundings* 101.2 (2018) 110–46.

Isasi-Díaz, Ada María. *Mujerista Theology: A Theology for the Twenty-First Century.* Maryknoll, NY: Orbis, 1996.

Jiménez, Pablo A. and Justo L. González. *Púlpito: An Introduction to Hispanic Preaching.* Nashville: Abingdon, 2005.

Johnson, Lyndon Baines. "Remarks at the Signing of the Immigration Bill." Speech, Liberty Island, NY, October 3, 1965. LBJ Presidential Library. http://www.lbjlibrary.org/lyndon-baines-johnson/timeline/lbj-on-immigration.

Kellerman, D. "גבר (*gvr*)." *The Theological Dictionary of the Old Testament.* Vol. 2 (Grand Rapids: Eerdmans, 1990.

"Key Facts on Individuals Eligible for the Deferred Action for Childhood Arrivals (DACA) Program." The Henry J. Kaiser Family Foundation. February 2018. http://files.kff.org/attachment/Fact-Sheet-Key-Facts-on-Individuals-Eligible-for-the-DACA-Program.

King, Martin Luther, Jr. "The One-Sided Approach of the Good Samaritan." Stanford University Dr. Martin Luther King, Jr. Research and Education Institute, November 20, 1955. https://kinginstitute.stanford.edu/king-papers/documents/one-sided-approach-good-samaritan/.

Koven, Steven G., and Frank Götzke. *American Immigration Policy: Confronting the Nation's Challenges.* New York: Springer, 2010.

Koehler, Ludwig and Walter Baumgartner, *The Hebrew and Aramaic Lexicon of the Old Testament.* Vol. 1. Leiden: Brill, 1994.

Krogstad, Jens Manuel, Jeffrey S. Passel, and D'Vera Cohn. "5 Facts about Illegal Immigration in the U.S." Pew Research Center. November 28, 2018. http://www.pewresearch.org/fact-tank/2018/11/28/5-facts-about-illegal-immigration-in-the-u-s.

Labor Council for Latin American Advancement (LCLAA), *Another America Is Possible: The Impact of NAFTA on the U.S. Latino Community and Lessons for Future Trade Agreements*, Product ID 9013. Washington, DC: Public Citizen's Global Trade Watch, 2004.

Lapide, Pinchas. *The Sermon on the Mount: Utopia or Program for Action?* Maryknoll, NY: Orbis, 1986.

Lee, Michelle Ye Hee. "Donald Trump's False Comments." *Washington Post.* https://www.washingtonpost.com/news/fact-checker/wp/2015/07/08/donald-trumps-false-comments-connecting-mexican-immigrants-and-crime/?noredirect=on.

Long, Thomas G. *The Witness of Preaching.* 2nd ed. Louisville: Westminster John Knox, 2005.

López, Ann Aurelia. *The Farmworkers' Journal.* Berkeley: University of California Press, 2007, 7–9, 41.

López, Gustavo, and Jens Manuel Krogstad. "Key Facts about Unauthorized Immigrants Enrolled in DACA." Pew Research Center. September 25, 2017. http://www.pewresearch.org/fact-tank/2017/09/25/key-facts-about-unauthorized-immigrants-enrolled-in-daca.

López, Gustavo, Kristen Bialik, and Jynnah Radford. "Key Findings about U.S. Immigrants." Pew Research Center. November 30, 2018. http://www.pewresearch.org/fact-tank/2018/11/30/key-findings-about-u-s-immigrants.

Lughood, Lila Abu. *Veiled Sentiments: Honor and Poetry in the Bedouin Society.* Berkeley: University of California, 1986.

Maduro, Otto. *Maps for a Fiesta: A Latina/o Perspective on Knowledge and the Global Crisis.* Introduction by Eduardo Mendieta. New York: Fordham University Press, 2015.

Magness, Josh. "He Ranted at Spanish Speakers: Protesters Threw a Latin-themed Party outside His Home." *Miami Herald,* May 19, 2018. https://www.miamiherald.com/news/nation-world/national/article211502129.html.

Mahmood, Saba. *Religious Difference in a Secular Age: A Minority Report.* Princeton: Princeton University Press, 2016.

Malina, Bruce J. "Hospitality." In *Handbook of Biblical Social Values,* edited by John J. Pilch and Bruce J. Malina, 96–99. 3rd ed. Matrix. Eugene, OR: Cascade Books, 2016.

"Manifest Destiny, Continued: President McKinley Defends U.S. Expansionism." http://historymatters.gmu.edu/d/5575.

Martin-Achard, R. "*gvr.*" *Theological Lexicon of the Old Testament*, edited by Ernst Jenni and Claus Westermann, 1:309. Translated by Mark E. Biddle. Peabody: Hendrickson, 1997.

Mbembe, Achille. *Critique of Black Reason.* A John Hope Franklin Center Book. Durham: Duke University Press, 201.

McClure, John S. "Preacher as Host and Guest." In *Slow of Speech and Unclean Lips: Contemporary Images of Preaching Identity,* edited by Robert Stephen Reid, 119–43. Eugene, OR: Cascade Books, 2010.

————. *The Roundtable Pulpit: Where Leadership and Preaching Meet.* Nashville: Abingdon, 1995.

McIntyre, Erin Siegal, and Deborah Bonello, "Is Rape the Price to Pay for Migrant Women Chasing the American Dream?" *Fusion*, September 10, 2014. http://fusion.net/story/17321/is-rape-the-price-to-pay-for-migrant-women-chasing-the-american-dream.

Mignolo, Walter D., and Catherine E. Walsh. *On Decoloniality: Concepts, Analytics, Praxis* Durham: Duke University Press, 2018.

Milgrom, Jacob. "The Alien in Your Midst." *The Bible Review.* 11:06, December 1995.

————. *Leviticus*, 2 Vols. The Anchor Yale Bible Commentary (New Haven: Yale, 2007).

Neville, David J. "Toward a Hermeneutic of Shalom: Reading Texts of Teleological Terror in Peace Perspective." *Word & World* 34 (2014) 339–48.

New York Times. "Government to Shut Down: House and Senate Adjourn with no Spending Deal." December 21, 2018.

Nichols, J. Randall. *The Restoring Word: Preaching as Pastoral Communication.* 1987. Reprint, Eugene, OR: Wipf & Stock, 2003.

Norflect, Agnes W. "One New Book for the Preacher." *The Journal for Preachers*, vol. 42.2 (2019) 45.

Obama, Barack. "Remarks by the President on Immigration." Speech, Rose Garden, Washington, DC, June 15, 2012. Obama White House Archives. https://obamawhitehouse.archives.gov/the-press-office/2012/06/15/remarks-president-immigration.

Oden, Amy G., ed. *And You Welcomed Me: A Sourcebook on Hospitality in Early Christianity.* Nashville: Abingdon, 2001.

Osbon, Abiathar M. "The Duty of America to Her Immigrant Citizens." New York: New York Conference, 1848.

Painter, Nell I. *The History of White People.* New York: Norton, 2010

Peterson, Richard D. "The Widow, the Orphan, and the Poor in the Old Testament and Extra-biblical Literature." *Bibliotheca Sacra* 130 (1973) 223–34.

Powery, Emerson. "Commentary on Mark 6:14–29." *Working Preacher,* July 15, 2018. https://www.workingpreacher.org/preaching.aspx?commentary_id=1325.

Plyler v. Doe 457 U.S. 202 (1982). http://www2.law.cornell.edu/cgi-bin/foliocgi.exe/historic/query.

Pohl, Christine D. *Making Room: Recovering Hospitality as a Christian Tradition.* Grand Rapids: Eerdmans, 1999.

Potter, Rockwell Harmon. "The Meaning of Victory and Peace." Sermon delivered at the First Church of Christ and the Second Church of Christ, Hartford, Connecticut, November 28, 1918.

Powell, John. *Immigration.* New York: Infobase, 2007.

Prudente, Tim. "Two Men, One Heart." *Baltimore Sun*, December 28, 2018. https://www.baltimoresun.com/health/bs-md-heart-donor-20181220-story.html.

Radford, Jynnah, and Abby Budiman. "Facts on U.S. Immigrants, 2016: Statistical Portrait of the Foreign-born Population in the United States." Pew Research Center. September 14, 2018. http://www.pewhispanic.org/2018/09/14/facts-on-u-s-immigrants-trend-data.

"Recent Adjudication: Asylum Law." *Harvard Law Review* 132 (2018) 803–10.

Rogers, Jeffrey S. "Texts of Terror and the Essence of Scripture: Encountering the Jesus of John 8: A Sermon on John 8:31–59." *Review & Expositor* 103 (2006) 205–12.

Rogers, Robert F. *Destiny's Landfall: A History of Guam.* Honolulu: University of Hawai'i Press, 1995.

Román, Reinaldo L. *Governing Spirits: Religion, Miracles, and Spectacles in Cuba and Puerto Rico, 1898–1956.* Chapel Hill: University of North Carolina Press, 2007.

Rose, Lucy Atkinson. *Sharing the Word: Preaching in the Roundtable Church.* Louisville, KY: Westminster John Knox, 1997.

Rusling, James "Interview with President William McKinley." *The Christian Advocate* 22 (January 1903) 17.

Sanders, Jack T. *Ethics in the New Testament.* Philadelphia: Fortress, 1975.

Schlabach, Gerald W. "'Confessional' Nonviolence and the Unity of the Church: Can Christians Square the Circle?" *Journal of the Society of Christian Ethics* 34 (2014) 125–44.

Shoop, Marcia Mount. *Let the Bones Dance: Embodiment and the Body of Christ.* Louisville: Westminster John Knox, 2010.

Spenser, John R. "Sojourner." In *The Anchor Yale Bible Dictionary,* edited by David Noel Freedman, 6:104. New Haven: Yale, 1992.

Su, Anna. *Exporting Freedom: Religious Liberty and American Power.* Cambridge: Harvard University Press, 2016.

Thompson, John L. "Preaching Texts of Terror in the Book of Judges: How Does the History of Interpretation Help?" *Calvin Theological Journal* 37 (2002) 49–61.

Tichenor, Daniel J. *Dividing Lines: The Politics of Immigration Control in America.* Princeton: Princeton University Press, 2002.

Tienda, Marta. "Multiplying Diversity: Family Unification and the Regional Origins of Late-Age US Immigrants." *International Migration Review* 51 (2017) 727–56. https://www.ncbi.nlm.nih.gov/pmc/articles/PMC5613757.

Times of Israel Staff and Agencies. "Bolton Warns Iran of 'Hell to Pay' in Impassioned NY Speech." *The Times of Israel.* Last updated Sept. 26, 2018. https://www.timesofisrael.com/bolton-to-warn-iran-of-hell-to-pay-in-impassioned-ny-speech/

Trible, Phyllis. *Texts of Terror: Literary-Feminist Readings of Biblical Narratives.* Overtures to Biblical Theology. Philadelphia: Fortress, 1984.

Truax, Eileen. *Dreamers: An Immigrant Generation's Fight for their American Dream.* Boston: Beacon, 2015.

United Nations Office of the High Commissioner of Human Rights. "Figures at a Glance." https://www.unhcr.org/figures-at-a-glance.html

———. "Migration and Human Rights: People on the Move." http://www.ohchr.org/EN/Issues/Migration/Pages/MigrationAndHumanRightsIndex.aspx

———. "With 1 human in every 113 affected, forced displacement hits record high." http://www.unhcr.org/en-us/news/press/2016/6/5763ace54/1-human-113-affected-forced-displacement-hits-record-high.html

United Nations High Commissioner for Refugees. "Global Trends: Forced Displacement in 2017." June 25, 2018. https://www.unhcr.org/en-us/statistics/unhcrstats/5b27be547/unhcr-global-trends-2017.html.

United States President. Presidential Determination. "Presidential Determination on Refugee Admissions for Fiscal Year 2019, Determination 2019–01 of October 4, 2018." Federal Register 83, No. 212 (November 1, 2018): 2018–24135. https://www.govinfo.gov/content/pkg/FR-2018-11-01/pdf/2018-24135.pdf.

United States Citizenship and Immigration Services. https://www.uscis.gov.

United States Department of Homeland Security. *U Visa Law Enforcement Certification Resource Guide for Federal, State, Local, Tribal, and Territorial Law Enforcement.* https://www.dhs.gov/xlibrary/assets/dhs_u_visa_certification_guide.pdf.

United States Department of State, United States Department of Homeland Security, and United States Department of Health and Human Services. *Proposed Refugee Admission for Fiscal Year 2019: Report to Congress.* Washington, DC, September 24, 2018. https://www.state.gov/documents/organization/286401.pdf.

United States. "Diversity Visa Program, DV 2016–2018: Number of Entries Received During Each Online Registration Period by Country of Chargeability." United States Department of State. https://travel.state.gov/content/dam/visas/Diversity-Visa/DVStatistics/DV%20AES%20statistics%20by%20FSC%202016–2018.pdf.

United States. *The Visa Bulletin.* U.S. Department of State, Bureau of Consular Affairs. https://travel.state.gov/content/travel/en/legal/visa-lawo/visa-bulletin.html.

United States. "Visa Bulletin For January 2019." United States Department of State, Bureau of Consular Affairs. https://travel.state.gov/content/travel/en/legal/visa-lawo/visa-bulletin/2019/visa-bulletin-for-january-2019.html.

United States. *Yearbook of Immigration Statistics.* Washington, D.C.: U.S. Department of Homeland Security, Office of Immigration Statistics, 2017. https://www.dhs.gov/immigration-statistics/yearbook/2017#*.

USCIS History Office and Library. *Overview of INS History.* United States Citizenship and Immigration Services. https://www.uscis.gov/sites/default/files/USCIS/History%20and%20Genealogy/Our%20History/INS%20History/INSHistory.pdf.

Vermes, Geza. *The Complete Dead Sea Scrolls in English.* New York: Penguin, 1997.

Wang, Amy B. "'My Next Call Is to ICE!': A Man Flipped out Because Workers Spoke Spanish at a Manhattan Deli." *Washington Post*, May 17, 2018. https://www.washingtonpost.com/news/business/wp/2018/05/16/my-next-call-is-to-ice-watch-a-man-wig-out-because-workers-spoke-spanish-at-a-manhattan-deli/?noredirect=on.

Warren, Robert. "US Undocumented Population Continued to Fall from 2016 to 2017, and Visa Overstays Significantly Exceeded Illegal Crossings for the Seventh Consecutive Year." Center for Migration Studies. January 16, 2019. https://doi.org/10.14240/cmsesy011619

Washington Post Staff. "Donald Trump Announces a Presidential Bid." June 16, 2015. https://www.washingtonpost.com/news/post-politics/wp/2015/06/16/full-text-donald-trump-announces-a-presidential-bid/?utm_term=.9ca56bc652e6.

Winston, Kimberly. "Report Says List of 'Islamophobic Groups' Reaches New High," *Religious News Service*, June 21, 2016, http://religionnews.com/2016/06/20/report-says-list-of-islamophobic-groups-reaches-new-high.

Wong, Tom K. *The Politics of Immigration.* New York: Oxford University Press, 2017.

Young, Carlton R., ed. *The United Methodist Hymnal.* Nashville: United Methodist Publishing House, 1989.

Zauzmer, Julie. "The Alleged Synagogue Shooter was a Churchgoer Who Talked Christian Theology, Raising Tough Questions for Evangelical Pastors." *The Washington Post*, May 1, 2019. https://www.washingtonpost.com/religion/2019/05/01/alleged-synagogue-shooter-was-churchgoer-who-articulated-christian-theology-prompting-tough-questions-evangelical-pastors/?utm_term=.cc882ad961bf.

Made in the USA
Coppell, TX
16 November 2020

41480934R00105